MICHIGAN

DAILY
DEVOTIONS
FOR
DIE-HARD
FANS

WOLVERINES

MICHIGAN

Daily Devotions for Die-Hard Fans: Michigan Wolverines
© 2012 Ed McMinn
Extra Point Publishers; P.O. Box 871; Perry, GA 31069

Library of Congress Cataloging-in-Publication Data
13 ISBN Digit ISBN: 978-0-9846377-7-5

Manufactured in the United States of America.

Unless otherwise noted, scripture quotations are taken from the *Holy Bible, New International Version*. Copyright © 1973, 1978, 1984, by the International Bible Society. All rights reserved.

Visit us at www.die-hardfans.com.

Cover and interior design by Slynn McMinn.

Every effort has been made to identify copyright holders. Any omissions are unintentional. Extra Point Publishers should be notified in writing immediately for full acknowledgement in future editions.

WOLVERINES

Hail to the Victors valiant,
Hail to the conquering heroes,
Hail, hail to Michigan
The leaders and best;

Hail to the Victors valiant,
Hail to the conquering heroes
Hail, hail to Michigan
The Champions of the West.

The following titles are available:

DAY 1

IN THE BEGINNING

Read Genesis 1, 2:1-3.

"God saw all that he had made, and it was very good" (v. 1:31).

In the beginning, a letter showed up.

In the fall of 1878, a letter addressed to the Michigan Foot-ball [*sic*] Association arrived on campus. It contained a challenge from the "foot-ball" team of Racine College and a quite generous offer. The Racine team would procure the field, pay for the advertising, and give the Michigan team two-thirds of the gate receipts. One big obstacle, though, made the game unlikely: Michigan didn't have a football team (or a foot-ball team).

Nevertheless, the challenge was accepted with the proviso that the game not be played until the spring, which would give the school time to prepare a team. How diligent those preparations were was a matter for discussion. In April 1879, the student newspaper proclaimed, "It is high time that our teams were hard at work every day. But they are not. Indeed they seem to be distinguished only by their laziness and lack of enthusiasm."

In May, though, the school's athletic association appointed a committee to select the players, pick uniforms, and raise money. Two weeks later, a team of twenty-two players had been selected.

The first intercollegiate football game in Michigan history was played on May 30, 1879, in Chicago against the Purple Stockings from Racine College. Twelve players represented Michigan, taking the train to Chicago and a bus to the playing field.

The game was more like rugby than today's football, played in two "innings" of 45 minutes each. In the first inning, Irving Kane Pond scored the first touchdown in UM football history. The rules required that the kick after touchdown be good before a point was allowed. The kick was missed.

In the second inning, though, John Chase scored and Michigan captain David DeTarr kicked the goal. Football at the University of Michigan had begun, fittingly enough, with a win, 1-0.

Beginnings are important, but what we make of them is even more important. Consider, for example, how far the University of Michigan football program has come since that first season.

Every morning of your life, you get a gift from God: a new beginning. God hands to you as an expression of divine love a new day full of promise and the chance to right the wrongs in your life. You can use the day to pay a debt, start a new relationship, replace a burned-out light bulb, tell your family you love them, chase a dream, solve a nagging problem . . . or not.

God simply provides the gift. How you use it is up to you. People often talk wistfully about starting over or making a new beginning. God gives you the chance with the dawning of every new day. You have the chance today to make things right – and that includes your relationship with God.

One very important point must not be overlooked. It is essential that we win the first game.
-- The student newspaper The Chronicle *in 1879*

Every day is not just a dawn; it is a precious chance to start over or begin anew.

SOMETHING NEW

Read Ephesians 4:17-24.

"You were taught . . . to put off your old self . . . and to put on the new self, created to be like God in true righteousness and holiness" (vv. 22, 24).

Michigan Stadium hosted its first-ever football game on Oct. 1, 1927. Almost eighty-four years later, The Big House was home to something new.

On Sept. 10, 2011, the largest crowd in college football history jammed the venerable facility for the first night game in its history. They got a game more than fitting for the historic occasion.

The loyal opposition the Night the Lights Went On in The Big House was provided by the Notre Dame Fighting Irish. The Wolverines apparently spent the first three quarters blinded by the light as Notre Dame led 24-7 with fifteen minutes to play. But junior quarterback Denard Robinson scored from the 1 and threw a 14-yard TD pass to sophomore wide receiver Jeremy Gallon to pull Michigan to within three.

After that, the Irish hung grimly on as the night got longer and the time got shorter. Then with only 1:12 left, Robinson threw a 21-yard touchdown pass to junior running back Vincent Smith. For the first time in the game, Michigan led, just in time, apparently, to have pulled out the win.

Not so fast. The Irish seemed to have saved themselves with a touchdown with only 30 seconds left. That made it 31-28. It wasn't time, though, to turn out the lights and go home. "When it's 0:00 on the clock, that's the only time the game is over," declared first-year UM head coach Brady Hoke.

Robinson promptly completed the longest pass of his college career, a 74-yard bomb to a wide-open Gallon that carried to the Irish 16. "Coach took a stab," said junior wide receiver Roy Round-tree about what happened next: Hoke went for the end zone. With 0:02 on the clock, Robinson found Roundtree with a TD pass.

For the Irish, the lights went out. Michigan won 35-31.

New things in our lives often have a life-changing effect. A new spouse. A new baby. A new job. Even something as mundane as a new television set or lawn mower jolts us with change.

While new experiences, new people, and new toys may make our lives new, they can't make new lives for us. Inside, where it counts – down in the deepest recesses of our soul – we're still the same, no matter how desperately we may wish to change.

An inner restlessness drives us to seek escape from a life that is a monotonous routine. Such a mundane existence just isn't good enough for someone who is a child of God; it can't even be called living. We want more out of life; something's got to change.

The only hope for a new life lies in becoming a brand new man or woman. And that is possible only through Jesus Christ, he who can make all things new again.

It was a heart-pounding, pom-pom pumping night under the lights at the Big House.
-- Associated Press on the 2011 Notre Dame game

A brand new you with the promise of a life worth living is waiting in Jesus Christ.

DAY 3

WHAT A SURPRISE!

Read 1 Thessalonians 5:1-11.

"But you, brothers, are not in darkness so that this day should surprise you like a thief" (v. 4).

Michigan gymnastics coach Kurt Golder was not pleased that this student thought he could just walk off the street and make the team. Boy, was Golder surprised.

David Chan was a senior cocaptain of the 2010 NCAA national champion men's gymnastics team. The incredible season capped off a remarkable career at Ann Arbor for Chan, who at one time or another earned All-American honors in the pommel horse and the vault. He was also a two-time Academic All-America.

A native of Singapore, Chan attended boarding school in Australia where he was involved with gymnastics. A three-year stint in the military, though, apparently put the sport behind him.

His military obligation completed, Chan applied to Michigan without ever seeing the campus and was accepted, arriving in the fall of 2007. He made friends easily and learned Michigan had a men's gymnastics team. He knew nothing about American college gymnastics, but he still loved the sport, so he was intrigued. He merely wanted to hop on the pommel horse or do a few flips to relive his glory days and have a little fun.

So he strolled into the gymnastics practice facility one day, met Golder, and asked him if he could just horse around a little. The coach's reply was not encouraging. "I had to set him straight

-- that's not how it works," he said. "If you're working out here, you're on the gymnastics team. We're not a drop-in kind of club."

The two chatted further, and Chan arranged a tryout with an assistant coach. Ten minutes into the tryout the assistant called Golder with the surprising news: This kid was really good.

Yes, he was, to everyone's surprise.

Surprise birthday parties are a delight. And what's the fun of opening Christmas presents when we already know what's in them? Some surprises in life provide us with experiences that are both joyful and delightful.

Generally, though, we expend energy and resources to avoid most surprises and the impact they may have upon our lives. We may be surprised by the exact timing of a baby's arrival, but we nevertheless have the bags packed beforehand and the nursery all set for its occupant. Paul used this very image (v. 3) to describe the Day of the Lord, when Jesus will return to claim his own and establish his kingdom. We may be caught by surprise, but we must still be ready.

The consequences of being caught unprepared by a baby's insistence on being born are serious indeed. They pale, however, beside the eternal effects of not being ready when Jesus returns. We prepare ourselves just as Paul told us to (v. 8): We live in faith, hope, and love, ever on the alert for that great, promised day.

I have to say I was surprised. All-American types of gymnasts just don't walk into your office off the street.
                                        -- Kurt Golder on David Chan

The timing of Jesus' return will be a surprise; the consequences should not be.

DAY 4

MAKE NO MISTAKE

Read Mark 14:66-72.

"Then Peter remembered the word Jesus had spoken to him: 'Before the rooster crows twice you will disown me three times.' And he broke down and wept" (v. 72).

A mistake involving a young equipment manager once kept Michigan from losing a football game.

Jon Falk joined Bo Schembechler's staff as equipment manager in 1974. As the program's Director of Equipment Operations, he has on more than one occasion been honored for excellence by his profession's national association.

In the 1975 game against Baylor, Michigan led 14-7 at halftime and kicked off to start the third quarter. Someone pointed out to Falk that a pylon was missing at the goal line toward which the Bears were driving. Whether the pylon had never been in place or whether Falk had originally set it in place and it had been taken or knocked loose didn't matter. It wasn't there now and it should have been.

A frantic Falk raced to the storage area and retrieved a pylon. Before he could make it to the field, though, Baylor's fullback was pushed out of bounds at the goal line. The referee looked down, didn't see a pylon, and waved off the touchdown. Michigan held.

As soon as the series was over, Falk ran over and set the pylon in place. According to Falk, the ref who had waved off the score looked at him like, "Hey, what's going on here?" Falk apologized, to the official, but the play stood. The game ended in a 14-14 tie rather than a 21-14 loss for Michigan.

An article in a Dallas newspaper said while the Baylor coaches were watching the game film, they saw Falk running down the sideline with a pylon in his hand. Head coach Grant Teaff said he saw it as an honest mistake. "I saw the kid on the film, and he was making an honest effort to get the pylon set," Teaff said.

It's distressing but it's true: Like football teams, equipment managers, and Simon Peter, we all make mistakes. Only one perfect man ever walked on this earth, and no one of us is he. Some mistakes are just dumb. Like locking yourself out of your car or falling into a swimming pool with your clothes on.

Other mistakes are more significant. Like heading down a path to addiction. Committing a crime. Walking out on a spouse and the children.

All these mistakes, however, from the momentarily annoying to the life-altering tragic, share one aspect: They can all be forgiven in Christ. Other folks may not forgive us; we may not even forgive ourselves. But God will forgive us when we call upon him in Jesus' name.

Thus, the twofold fatal mistake we can make is ignoring the fact that we will die one day and subsequently ignoring the fact that Jesus is the only way to shun Hell and enter Heaven. We absolutely must get this one right.

I wasn't trying to cheat anybody. I just couldn't make it fast enough.
-- Jon Falk on correcting the mistake of the missing pylon

Only one mistake we make sends us to Hell when we die: ignoring Jesus while we live.

DAY 5

SMART MOVE

Read 1 Kings 4:29-34; 11:1-6.

*"[Solomon] was wiser than any other man. . . . As
Solomon grew old, his wives turned his heart after other
gods, and his heart was not fully devoted to the Lord his
God" (vv. 4:31, 11:4).*

The head coach agreed to a suggestion from an assistant and made what is surely the smartest move in UM football history.

From 1938-47, Fritz Crisler won 71 games and lost 16, a winning percentage topped in school history only by Fielding Yost among Michigan coaches with longevity. He had on his staff a perceptive assistant coach named Bennie Oosterbaan, who followed him as head coach from 1948-58 and won 63 games.

What Oosterbaan saw prior to the 1938 season was a talented player named Paul Kromer, who was slated to be the team's tailback. That is, Kromer was to be the team's primary ball carrier. A contemporary described Kromer as a "great, great football player." He led the team in pass receiving and scoring in 1938.

But what Oosterbaan also saw was the guy penciled in as the team's starting wingback, a position that called for more pass receiving than running the ball. The assistant coach thought that the wingback would make a better tailback, and vice versa. So he suggested the switch to Crisler, who approved the move.

The result is quite literally Michigan legend.

The player originally slated to be a pass receiver rather than a

WOLVERINES

running back was Tom Harmon, perhaps still the most famous and revered player in Wolverine football history. Old No. 98 led the team in passing, rushing, and total offense his three varsity seasons (1938-40). He led the nation in scoring his last two years and was All-America both seasons. He capped off his remarkable career in 1940 by wining the Heisman Trophy.

All because his head coach made a smart move.

Remember that time you wrecked the car when you spilled hot coffee on your lap? That cold morning you fell out of the boat? The time you gave your honey a tool box for her birthday?

Formal education notwithstanding, we all make some dumb moves sometimes because time spent in a classroom is not an accurate gauge of common sense. Folks impressed with their own smarts often grace us with erudite pronouncements that we intuitively recognize as flawed, unworkable, or simply wrong.

A good example is the observation that great intelligence and scholarship are inherently incompatible with a deep and abiding faith in God. That is, the more we know, the less we believe. Any incompatibility occurs, however, only because we begin to trust in our own wisdom rather than the wisdom of God. We forget, as Solomon did, that God is the ultimate source of all our knowledge and wisdom and that even our ability to learn is a gift from God.

Not smart at all.

I don't hire anybody not brighter than I am. If they're not smarter than me, I don't need them.

-- Bear Bryant

Being truly smart means trusting in God's wisdom rather than only in our own knowledge.

DAY 6

THE LAST WORD

Read Luke 9:22-27.

"The Son of Man ... must be killed and on the third day be raised to life. ... [S]ome who are standing here will ... see the kingdom of God" (vv. 22, 27).

Bo Schembechler once had the last word with an official without ever raising his voice or lapsing into profanity.

Schembechler, of course, is a Michigan and a college football legend. From 1969-1989, he coached the Wolverines to 194 wins, the most of any coach. He never had a losing season; during the 1970s, the Wolverines had the best record of any Division I team.

It was said of Schembechler that he had "a fiery disposition" and that he "was prone to sideline outbursts." During the five years Schembechler served as an assistant for Woody Hayes, the two intense, headstrong coaches frequently wound up yelling and kicking chairs at each other. Schembechler often related that Hayes repeatedly fired him after their fiery confrontations, only to rehire him when their tempers cooled down.

Jerry Hanlon was the only assistant coach to serve on Schembechler's staff his entire 21 years at Michigan. Despite the head man's "legendary volcanic personality, he "very seldom hollered at officials," Hanlon said. "He would talk to them when an official walked close to the bench." In other words, Schembechler voiced his displeasure but chose the moment for maximum effectiveness.

Hanlon said once, though, that the most scathing remark he

ever heard his boss make to an official was made after the game was over in a normal speaking voice and without benefit of any four-letter words.

Against Wisconsin one year, "the officiating was bad," according to Hanlon. "We were all mad." The Wolverines were walking off the field, and an official was walking in front of them when, as Hanlon remembered it, Schembechler said to the ref, "You walk like a girl."

That day, Bo Schembechler indeed had the last word.

Why is it that, unlike Bo Schembechler, we often come up with the last word – the perfect zinger -- only long after the incident that called for a smart and pithy rejoinder is over? "Man, I shoulda said that! That woulda fixed his wagon!" But it's too late.

Nobody in history, though, including us, could ever hope to match the man who had the greatest last word of them all: Jesus Christ. His enemies killed him and put him in a tomb, confident they were done with that nuisance for good. Instead, they were unwitting participants in God's great plan of redemption and gave the last word to Jesus. He has it still.

Jesus didn't go to that cross so he could die; he went to that cross so all those who follow him might live. Because of Jesus' own death on the cross, the final word for us is not our own death. Rather it is life, through our salvation in Jesus Christ.

It was the biggest put-down I may have ever heard from [Bo Schembechler] to an official.

-- *Jerry Hanlon*

**With Jesus, the last word is always life
and never death.**

MICHIGAN

DAY 7

GREAT EXPECTATIONS

Read John 1:43-51.

*"'Nazareth! Can anything good come from there?'
Nathanael asked" (v. 46).*

Expectations for this particular batch of Wolverines were that they would finish in the middle of the Big Ten pack. At the time, those predictions seemed pretty reasonable.

For one thing, the starting quarterback was a former walk-on and fifth-year senior who until spring practice had decided to give up football. That would be Brian Griese, who had started some games the season before only because the starter, Scott Dreisbach, had been injured.

The offensive line was a problem because of its youth. Senior Zach Adami and junior tackle Jon Jansen were the only proven returning starters, and Adami was being moved from guard to center. Tackle Jeff Backus, a redshirt freshman, was trying to return from a ruptured appendix and the subsequent loss of thirty-seven pounds. Sophomores and redshirts were contending for the other positions up front.

While the defensive front was fast and experienced, it was generally considered too light. Only senior defensive end Glen Steele looked solid. Unquestionably, the defensive backfield, led by All-American Charles Woodson, was the strength of the team. The defense was in good hands with coordinator Jim Herrmann, but this bunch "didn't look much like a Michigan defense from the vintage years."

Concerns also swirled about the head coach, Lloyd Carr. He had joined Bo Schembechler's staff in 1980 and had succeeded Gary Moeller after the 1994 season. But Carr had a big problem: He had lost four games in each of his first two years as the head man.

So the expectations were that this team was a middle-of-the-pack bunch. So did they meet those expectations? Not at all. This was the 1997 squad. They were national champions.

The blind date your friend promised would look like Brad Pitt or Jennifer Aniston but resembled a Munster or Cousin Itt. Your vacation that went downhill after the lost luggage. Often your expectations are raised only to be dashed. Sometimes it's best not to get your hopes up; then at least you have the possibility of being surprised.

Worst of all, perhaps, is when you realize that you are the one not meeting others' expectations. The fact is, though, that you aren't here to live up to what others think of you. Jesus didn't; in part, that's why they killed him. But he did meet God's expectations for his life, which was all that really mattered.

Because God's kingdom is so great, God does have great expectations for any who would enter, and you should not take them lightly. What the world expects from you is of no importance; what God expects from you is paramount.

Another four-loss season did not seem out of the question.
-- Writer George Cantor on expectations for the '97 season

You have little if anything to gain from meeting the world's expectations of you; you have all of eternity to gain from meeting God's.

DAY 8

A SECOND CHANCE

Read John 7:53-8:11.

"'Then neither do I condemn you,' Jesus declared. 'Go now and leave your life of sin'" (v. 8:11).

Shawn Hunwick got a second chance to bail his team out of a jam -- after he'd already done it once.

Hunwick completed his ice-hockey career at Michigan in 2012 as one of the program's best-ever goalies. He is UM's all-time leader in goals against average and save percentage.

In 2009-10, Hunwick rode the bench as a sophomore while UM finished seventh in the league. The only way the team could make a record 20th-straight appearance in the NCAA Tournament was to win six league playoff games, which had never been done before. After junior starter Bryan Hogan was sidelined by a torn muscle, the Wolverines had to win those games with a walk-on goalie who had never started a game. That would be Hunwick.

The Wolverines won those six games. Hunwick was the tournament MVP.

In the fall of 2010, Hunwick alternated with Hogan at goal, but when coach Red Berenson picked a goalie to play in the Big Chill before the largest crowd ever to watch a hockey game, he went with Hogan. During warm-ups, however, Hogan pulled a muscle. Hunwick skated to the rescue a second time. With no warm-up and no preparation, he shut out Michigan State 5-0.

Given a second chance to show what he could do, Hunwick led

the Wolverines on a run that included ending the season with an eight-game win streak. The team won the league championship, snatching it away from Notre Dame on the last night of play.

Michigan won the regional; Hunwick was the MVP. He then shut out North Dakota, considered the nation's top team, in the final four, before UM lost in overtime in the finals.

As one writer said, amid all those stars and future NHLers in the final four, "the best player on the ice was the 5-foot-6 walk-on goalie who didn't even have a full scholarship."

"If I just had a second chance, I know I could make it work out." Ever said that? If only you could go back and tell your dad one last time you love him, take that job you passed up rather than relocate, or replace those angry shouts at your son with gentle encouragement. If only you had a second chance, a mulligan.

As the story of Jesus' encounter with the adulterous woman illustrates, with God you always get a second chance. No matter how many mistakes you make, God will never give up on you. Nothing you can do puts you beyond God's saving power. You always have a second chance because with God your future is not determined by your past or who you used to be. It is determined by your relationship with God through Jesus Christ.

God is ready and willing to give you a second chance – or a third chance or a fourth chance – if you will give him a chance.

I've never seen any athlete get two chances to play Cinderella -- and [Shawn] Hunwick nailed it, both times.
> -- *John U. Bacon,* Ann Arbor Chronicle *columnist*

**You get a second chance with God
if you give him a chance.**

DAY 9

WHO, ME?

Read Judges 6:11-23.

"'But Lord,' Gideon asked, 'how can I save Israel? My clan is the weakest in Manasseh, and I am the least in my family'" (v. 15).

Ed Shannon was all set to hold for the extra point as he always did when -- to his shock -- the kicker told him to kick it.

From 1954-56, Shannon was a wingback for the Wolverines of Bennie Oosterbaan. He also played some at fullback and crossed the line to see some action as a linebacker.

Shannon made the traveling squad as a third-string wingback in 1954, but the All-Big Ten starter, Tony Branoff, and the backup, Ed Hickey, went down with injuries in the second and third games. Early in the week before the next game, Oosterbaan walked up to his third-stringer and announced, "Shannon, you are all we've got left." Thus did Shannon get his first start, against Northwestern.

Teammates in high school, Shannon and Wolverine quarterback Jim Maddock were old hands at changing up plays. In one prep game, they broke the huddle to punt with ten seconds left in the half when Shannon said to Maddock, "Why don't you run it?" "Ten seconds left, what could happen?" was Maddock's response. What happened was a 50-yard run around end for a touchdown.

Still, Shannon wasn't prepared for what Maddock pulled on him in the Army game of 1955. That season, Shannon held for the extra points and Maddock kicked. The huddle call was simple:

"Shannon hold, Maddock kick. Center when ready." When Shannon opened his fingers, the center snapped the ball.

After Michigan's second TD in the 26-2 win, Maddock called, "Maddock hold. Shannon kick. Center when ready." To Shannon's surprise, Maddock then dropped to one knee when the huddle broke. The two wound up arguing on the field about who was going to kick the PAT. Maddock won out, and Shannon "kicked a spiral that went banana-shape over the crossbar."

You probably know exactly how Ed Shannon felt; you've experienced that moment of unwelcome surprise with its sinking "who, me?" feeling. How about that time the teacher called on you when you hadn't done a lick of homework? Or the night the hypnotist pulled you out of a room full of folks to be his guinea pig? You've had the wide-eyed look and the turmoil in your midsection when you were suddenly singled out and found yourself in a situation you neither sought nor were prepared for.

You may feel exactly as Gideon did about being called to serve God in some way, quailing at the very notion of being audacious enough to teach Sunday school, coordinate a high school prayer club, or lead a small group study. Who, me? Hey, who's worthy enough to do anything like that?

The truth is that nobody is – but that doesn't seem to matter to God. And it's his opinion, not yours, that counts.

My scoring experience at the University of Michigan was 19 points, but that point is the one I will remember the rest of my life.
-- Ed Shannon on his 'Who-Me?' PAT

You're right in that no one is worthy to serve God, but the problem is that doesn't matter to God.

DAY 10

COMEBACK KIDS

Read Luke 23:26-43.

"Jesus answered him, 'I tell you the truth, today you will be with me in paradise'" (v. 43).

The Wolverines needed 31 points to pull off the biggest fourth-quarter comeback in school history.

On Oct. 10, 2003, the 100th meeting between Michigan and Minnesota was a blowout for three quarters with the 13th-ranked Golden Gophers acting as the really big wind. They led Michigan 28-7 and were coasting.

But in the first minute of the last period, senior quarterback John Navarre hit senior All-American running back Chris Perry with a 10-yard touchdown toss. Only 1:24 later, soph safety Jacob Stewart intercepted a pass and took it 34 yards for a touchdown.

Suddenly, with most of the fourth quarter still to go, the Wolverines trailed by only seven points.

The Gophers didn't burrow into a hole, though, scoring to make it a 35-21 game. Undaunted, Michigan continued its unheard-of comeback when Navarre teamed with All-Big Ten split end Braylon Edwards on a 52-yard bomb with 10:18 to play.

The defense held, setting the offense up 60 yards away from a tie with just over eight minutes left. An 18-yard pass from Navarre to Perry set up Perry's 10-yard touchdown run two plays later. Incredibly, the game was deadlocked at 35 with 5:48 on the clock.

The defense stood tall again, forcing a three-and-out. Michigan

WOLVERINES

took over at its own 42, and the last drive of the biggest comeback in the program's history began. The offense moved deliberately, carefully milking the clock until Navarre took a knee at the Minnesota 14. Garrett Rivas trotted out and booted a 33-yard field goal with 47 seconds left for the 38-35 win.

"I've never been in a game like this," Perry said. No one ever had in the long and storied history of Michigan football.

Life will have its setbacks whether they result from personal failures or from forces and people beyond your control. Being a Christian and a faithful follower of Jesus Christ doesn't insulate you from getting into deep trouble. Maybe financial problems suffocated you. A serious illness put you on the sidelines. Or your family was hit with a great tragedy.

Life is a whole series of victories and defeats. Ultimately, winning isn't about avoiding defeat; it's about getting back up to compete again. It's about making a comeback of your own.

When you avail yourself of God's grace and God's power, your comeback is always greater than your setback. You are never too far behind, and it's never too late in life's game for Jesus to lead you to victory, to turn trouble into triumph. As it was with the Wolverines against Minnesota in 2003 and the thief on the cross who repented, it's not how you start that counts; it's how you finish.

It just speaks to the human spirit, and those kids showed tremendous spirit.
-- UM Head coach Lloyd Carr on the comeback win over Minnesota

In life, victory is truly a matter of how you finish and whether you finish with Jesus at your side.

DAY 11

FIRED UP

Read Hebrews 3:13-19.

"Exhort one another every day, as long as it is called 'today,' so that none of you may be hardened by the deceitfulness of sin" (v. 13 NRSV).

Letters to the editor complained about them. They were booed by the students. A can of soda thrown from the stands hit one of them. Who were these awful people? The first female students at Michigan who dared to be cheerleaders.

In September 1974, the *Ann Arbor News* and the *Detroit News* proclaimed, "A U-M Tradition Crumbles!" That tradition was the all-male cheerleading squad at UM. Women were to be allowed on the sidelines that fall.

"There was some resentment," admitted Clare Canham-Eaton, a member of the initial group. "Resentment" is putting it somewhat mildly. The situation got so bad that two security guards accompanied the women anytime they were together.

The rules indicated the attitude toward the female troupe. They couldn't call themselves "cheerleaders"; rather, they were "pom-pom girls." They had to stay on one side of the field and weren't allowed to mingle with the boys. They couldn't initiate a cheer but could only join in after the guys started one. They were not allowed to ever let go of their pom-poms; never mind that holding them for four hours on game day colored their skin blue.

The women were officially designated as part of the band so no one would confuse them with the real cheerleaders. This segregation actually helped because band director George Cavender was supportive. He saw them as another entertainment avenue and drew up special numbers for them and rehearsed them.

It didn't take long for the malcontents to realize that having a group of lovely coeds on the sidelines cheering for their football team wasn't such a bad idea after all. "By the end of the year," said Canham-Eaton, "there was no controversy."

It's been a long, hard day. That couch at home is calling, but your desk is stacked with work. You're exhausted. And suddenly they show up: your personal cheerleading team. They dance, cheer, shout, wave pompoms, and generally exhort you to more and greater effort. They fire you up. That would work, wouldn't it? If only . . .

But you do have just such a squad in the most important aspect of your life: your faith. You have a big, ever growing bunch of folks who, if you will only surround yourself with them, will urge you on to a deeper, stronger relationship with Christ and to more abiding trust in God.

Who are these cheerleaders? They are your fellow believers in Christ. They come in teams -- called churches -- and they are exhorters who keep each other "in the game" that is faith. Christians are cheerleaders for God—and for God's team.

We were breaking tradition and making tradition at the same time.
– Clare Canham-Eaton on the first female cheerleaders at UM

**In the people of your church,
you have your own set of cheerleaders
who urge you to greater faithfulness.**

DAY 12

DRY RUN

Read John 4:1-15.

"Everyone who drinks this water will be thirsty again,
but whoever drinks the water I give him will never thirst.
Indeed, the water I give him will become in him a spring
of water welling up to eternal life" (vv. 13-14).

The Wolverines had to wait until they returned to Ann Arbor to learn that the drought was over.

On March 4, 2012, the Michigan men's basketball team took to the court in State College to try to do something that had not been accomplished in 26 long years: win a share of the Big Ten title.

As unlikely as it sounds, the last Michigan men's team to win the league title was back in 1986. That squad went 28-5 overall, 14-4 in the league. Bill Frieder was the head coach; Roy Tarpley and Butch Wade were the team captains. Since then, UM had made twelve trips to the NCAA Tournament, had won a national title (1989), and had been the national runner-up twice (1992 and 1993). But they had not won a regular season conference title.

As the 2011-12 season unwound and the Wolverines kept winning, head coach John Beilein deflected any talk of a league title -- until the last month when he finally admitted he had to talk to his team about it. "You do the math and you see right away that we have a great opportunity here," he said.

That opportunity was still there when the Wolverines took on Penn State in the last game of the regular season. A win and a

WOLVERINES

Michigan State loss would propel UM into a share of the title.

Michigan took care of business at its end. Behind 19 points from freshman point guard Trey Burke, the 13-ranked Wolverines took a 19-point lead in the second half and fought off a ferocious Penn State comeback for a 71-65 win. Not until they were back in Ann Arbor, though, hours later, did the players learn that Ohio State had beaten the Spartans.

The drought was over. They were Big Ten champions.

You can walk across that river you boated on in the spring. The city's put all neighborhoods on water restriction. That beautiful lawn you fertilized and seeded will turn a sickly, pale green and may lapse all the way to brown. Somebody wrote "Wash Me" on the rear window of your truck.

The sun bakes everything, including the concrete. The earth itself seems exhausted, just barely hanging on. It's a drought.

It's the way a soul that shuts God out looks.

God instilled the physical sensation of thirst in us to warn us of our body's need for water. He also gave us a spiritual thirst that can be quenched only by his presence in our lives. Without God, we are like tumbleweeds, dried out and windblown, offering the illusion of life where there is only death.

Living water – water of life – is readily available in Jesus. We may drink our fill, and thus we slake our thirst and end our soul's drought – forever.

You go into it (knowing the stakes), and we talked a lot about it. This is what champions do on this day.
         -- John Beilein on the title-clinching win over Penn State

Our soul thirsts for God's refreshing presence.

DAY 13

A FAST START

Read Acts 2:40-47.

"Everyone was filled with awe. . . . [They] ate together
with glad and sincere hearts, praising God and enjoying
the favor of all the people" (vv. 43a, 46b, 47a)

Errick Anderson did not exactly get off to a fast start at Michigan. In fact, early on in his freshman year, Bo Schembechler called him "the worst player we have ever recruited."

Anderson was a freshman fullback in the fall of 1988. At an early preseason scrimmage he went in to block for Jamie Morris, who still holds the Michigan record for all-purpose yards with 6,201. Morris was also the only player in history to lead the Wolverines in rushing four times until Mike Hart did so (2004-2007). So Morris was the star who must be protected.

But Anderson went the wrong way on the play. Schembechler went nuts when it ended, screaming, "Who's the fullback? Who's the fullback?" Anderson raised his hand. "Get out of here," the head coach barked. "I don't want you back in here until you know what you're doing. Get out of my huddle."

Anderson got. But he went back in on a play that he was sure he knew. He drove the linebacker back, but when the whistle blew, he turned around to see Schembechler picking Morris up off the ground in the backfield. He had blocked the wrong guy again.

When Schembechler saw Anderson had been the fullback on the play, he told him to "get on State Street and keep running until you hit 94, take a right, and don't stop until you hit Chicago." He called Anderson their worst player ever and added, "I don't know why we're wasting our money on you."

After Anderson's slow start, though, the money was anything but wasted on him. He was redshirted and then moved to inside linebacker where he blossomed. He was the first player in Michigan history to lead the team in tackles for four straight seasons. As an All-America in 1991, he became the first Wolverine ever to win the Butkus Award as the nation's best linebacker.

Fast starts are crucial for more than football games and races. Any time we begin something new, we want to get out of the gate quickly and jump ahead of the pack and stay there. We build up momentum from a fast start and keep rolling.

This is true for our faith life also. For a time after we accepted Christ as our savior, we were on fire with a zeal that wouldn't let us rest, much like the early Christians described in Acts. All too many Christians, however, let that blaze die down until only old ashes remain. We become lukewarm pew sitters.

The Christian life shouldn't be that way. Just because we were tepid yesterday doesn't mean we can't be boiling today. Every day we can turn to God for a spiritual tune-up that will put a new spark in our faith life; with a little tending that spark can soon become a raging fire. Today could be the day our faith life gets off to a fast start – again.

It was very intimidating. It was hard, and at times I was ready to leave.
-- Erick Anderson on his early days at Michigan

**Every day offers us a chance to get off
to a fast start for Jesus.**

DAY 14

IN THE KNOW

Read John 4:19-26, 39-42.

"They said to the woman, . . . 'Now we have heard for ourselves, and we know that this man really is the Savior of the world'" (v. 42).

Mike Hart was "eerily confident" about his team's chances against second-ranked Notre Dame. He just knew Michigan was going to win.

On Sept. 16, 2006, the 11th-ranked Wolverines trotted into the house that Rockne built as serious underdogs. They strutted out of the place with a newfound respect after they waxed the Irish 47-21. Michigan's "seriously ornery defense" held Notre Dame to four yards rushing and forced five turnovers.

On the other side of the ball, sophomore wide receiver Mario Manningham, the Big Ten's Offensive Player of the Week, caught four passes from quarterback Chad Henne for 137 yards and three touchdowns. The last score wound up slightly injuring Manningham when he collided with a female clarinetist from the Michigan Marching Band. "He pretty much knocked the wind out of me," she said. Manningham wound up with a bruised left wrist that sidelined him for a series. That led a sportswriter to comment that Michigan's band "had more success slowing [Manningham] down than did Notre Dame's secondary."

While the win clearly came as a surprise to many of the so-called experts, Hart, the team's star running back who had 124 yards rushing, knew it was coming. He had spent the week asking his teammates, "Do you feel it? Do you feel what I'm feeling?"

He later said that by game time his "feeling" had morphed into a conviction -- and he wasn't alone. "We knew we were gonna come down here and win this game," he said. "We knew."

Hart also knew Manningham would have a big day. While he was studying film, he called the Irish safeties "real nosy" in that they "nose[d] their way up into the box. I knew we'd be taking some shots."

The Wolverines just knew -- and Notre Dame was clueless.

The Michigan players just knew in the same way you know certain things in your life. That your spouse loves you, for instance. That you are good at your job. That this is a great country. That a bad day fishing is still better than a good day at work. You know these things even though no mathematician or philosopher can prove any of this on paper.

It's the same way with faith in Jesus: You just know that he is God's son and the savior of the world. You know it in the same way that you know Michigan is the only team worth pulling for: with every fiber of your being, with all your heart, your mind, and your soul. You know it despite the mindless babble and blasphemy of the unbelievers.

You just know, and because you know him, Jesus knows you. And that is all you really need to know.

Last year they were hunting us. This year we were hunting them.
-- Mike Hart on how he knew Michigan would beat Notre Dame

A life of faith is lived in certainty and conviction:
You just know you know.

DAY 15

DEAD WRONG

Read Matthew 26:14-16; 27:1-10.

"When Judas, who had betrayed him, saw that Jesus was condemned, he was seized with remorse" (v. 27:3).

Elroy Hirsch really did have this running business all wrong.

After a season of football at Wisconsin in 1942, Hirsch's commitment to the Navy's V-12 program required he transfer to Michigan. He played two seasons at running back for the Wolverines and was All-America in 1943. That school year he earned the distinction of being the only athlete in school history to letter in four sports in a single year.

When his military assignment kept Hirsch from making trips back to Madison to see his sweetheart, he solved the problem by joining the basketball team. "It was the only way he could get to Madison to see me," his future wife said. As the starting center, he led the conference in rebounding.

In the spring of 1944, Hirsch pitched the Wolverine baseball team to the Big Ten championship and was a star long jumper on Coach Ken Doherty's league champion track and field team.

Hirsch's unique running style made him a master in the art of broken field running on the gridiron. It also earned him one of sport's most enduring and endearing nicknames. A sportswriter for the *Chicago Daily News* said of Hirsch as he ran, "His crazy legs were gyrating in six different directions, all at the same time; he looked like a demented duck."

WOLVERINES

It was Doherty, however, who discovered that Hirsch's legs really were crazy. That broken field running that was so great on the football field kept Hirsch from staying in his lane on the track. Doherty felt that his star would be more effective if he would just run straight. When Doherty examined Hirsch's cleat marks, he saw the problem. "While Hirsch's right foot remained straight, his left toed inward. When he brought the leg back, it flew off on a wide tangent, sending him veering off-course."

Crazylegs Hirsch really did run the wrong way.

There's wrong, there's dead wrong, and there's Judas wrong. We've all been wrong in our lives, but we can at least honestly ease our conscience by telling ourselves we'll never be as wrong as Judas was. A close examination of Judas' actions, however, reveals that we can indeed replicate in our own lives the mistake Judas made that drove him to suicidal despair.

Judas ultimately regretted his betrayal of our Lord, but his sorrow and remorse, however boundless, could not save him. His attempt to undo his initial wrong was futile because he tried to fix everything himself rather than turning to God in repentance and begging for mercy.

While we can't literally betray Jesus to his enemies as Judas did, we can match Judas' failure in our own lives by not turning to God in Jesus' name and asking for forgiveness for our sins. In that case, we ultimately will be as dead wrong as Judas was.

I must've looked pretty funny.
-- Elroy 'Crazylegs' Hirsch on his running style

**A sin is the first wrong; failing to ask God
for forgiveness of it is the second.**

DAY 16

DIVIDED LOYALTIES

Read Matthew 6:1-24.

"No one can serve two masters" (v. 24a).

For Carmen Reynolds, the decision to play basketball at Michigan was an easy one. For her family, though, it created all sorts of serious problems about where their loyalties lay.

Reynolds grew up practically on the back porch of the Ohio State campus. Her family received a Christmas card every year from Jim Tressel when he was the Buckeye head football coach. An older brother played lacrosse for OSU. Christmas photos of the family showed them all draped in their Buckeye colors.

As Carmen became a basketball star, her parents began to consider the unheard-of and rather horrifying possibility that she might actually wind up a Wolverine. During her sophomore year, they asked Carmen what she would do if Michigan were the only school to offer her a scholarship. "I guess I would be a Michigan Wolverine," she replied. She then turned the tables on her folks, asking them what they would do. They answered, "We would be the biggest Michigan fans in the world!"

Sure enough, that exact scenario played out. Ohio State wasn't interested and Michigan offered a scholarship. Nevertheless, Carmen didn't rule out other offers until the three of them made a trip to Ann Arbor. When they went into a store and bought armloads of maize and blue apparel, the decision was made.

As Carmen entered her senior year of high school in 2007, the

WOLVERINES

Reynolds family was officially a clan with divided loyalties. "It was crazy to think that Carmen would be attending that 'School up North,'" her brother said. But even the Buckeye lacrosse player switched to maize and blue when he went to Carmen's games.

There were a lot of them, 119 to be exact from 2008-11. The guard/forward started every game her last three years at Michigan and scored 1,167 points, which left her name in the record book as the 13th leading scorer in the program's history.

You probably understand very well the stress that comes along with divided loyalties. The Christian work ethic drives you to be successful. The world, however, often makes demands and presents images that conflict with your devotion to God: movies deride God; couples play musical beds in TV sitcoms; and TV dramas portray Christians as killers following God's orders.

It's Sunday morning and the office will be quiet or the golf course won't be crowded. What do you do when your heart and loyalties are pulled in two directions? Jesus knew of the struggle we face; that's why he spoke of not being able to serve "two masters," that we wind up serving one and despising the other. Put in terms of either serving God or despising God, the choice is stark and clear.

Your loyalty is to God -- always.

[My family is] flying one of those 'house divided' flags, which is pretty cool. My uncle even wore a gray sweatshirt with a little block 'M' on it.
-- Carmen Reynolds on her family's divided loyalties

God does not condemn you for being successful
and enjoying popular culture, but your loyalty
must lie first and foremost with him.

DAY 17

THE SCAPEGOAT

Read Leviticus 16:15-22.

*"He is to lay both hands on the head of the live goat and
confess over it all the wickedness and rebellion of the
Israelites — all their sins — and put them on the goat's
head" (v. 21).*

Like the plot of a bad science fiction movie, a goat was geneti-
cally altered and a football hero emerged." That goat/hero was
Fred Trosko.

Trosko was a multi-sport star for the Wolverines from 1937-39,
earning nine letters in football, basketball, and baseball. He was a
starter at halfback for three seasons.

Against Ohio State in 1939, though, Trosko was undoubtedly
the game's goat as far as the Wolverines were concerned. His first-
down fumble led to a Buckeye touchdown. Three minutes later, a
Trosko pass was intercepted, which led to a second OSU score. "It
was 14-0, thanks solely to Trosko's two costly mistakes."

But Tom Harmon -- "the greatest football player the University
of Michigan has ever seen" -- led a rally. In the second quarter, the
1940 Heisman-Trophy winner hit end Joe Rogers with a 44-yard
pass that set up a touchdown toss to Forest Evashevski, who was
enshrined in the College Football Hall of Fame as a coach in 2000.
Harmon kicked the extra point. He then scored from 16 yards out,
again kicking the PAT, and the game was tied at 14.

That's where the score stayed as the two teams traded punts

until Harmon led a late Michigan drive. With only 50 seconds to play, UM faced fourth down at the OSU 24. Head coach Fritz Crisler turned to the Wolverine goat to pull off a miracle.

Trosko trotted back onto the field and knelt to field the snap for a Harmon field goal. But when he got the ball, Trosko stood up, turned the corner, and went untouched for the game-winning TD.

As Trosko left the field, Michigan Stadium broke into wild, unrestrained applause. The goat had become the hero.

A particular type of goat -- a scapegoat – could really be useful. Mess up at work? Bring him in to get chewed out. Make a decision your children don't like? Let him put up with the whining and complaining. Forget your anniversary? Call him in to grovel.

What a set-up! You don't have to pay the price for your mistakes, your shortcomings, and your failures. You get off scot-free. Exactly the way forgiveness works with Jesus.

Our sins separate us from God because we the unholy can't stand in the presence of the holy God. To remove our guilt, God requires a blood sacrifice. Out of his unimaginable love for us, he provided the sacrifice: his own son. Jesus is the sacrifice made for us; through Jesus and Jesus alone, forgiveness and eternity with God are ours.

It's a bumper sticker, but it's true: We aren't perfect; we're just forgiven.

I never blame myself when I'm not hitting. I just blame the bat, and if it keeps up, I change bats.

– Yogi Berra

For all those times you fail God, you have Jesus to take the guilt and the blame for you.

DAY 18

GLORY DAYS

Read Colossians 3:1-4.

*"When Christ, who is your life, appears, then you also
will appear with him in glory" (v. 4).*

Tommy Hendricks had his moments of glory as a Wolverine
safety, but only one landed him on ESPN -- twice.

The 1999 season opener against Notre Dame was yet another
classic in the storied rivalry. The Irish led 22-19 when senior quarterback Tom Brady led the Wolverines on a 58-yard scoring drive
culminated by tailback Anthony Thomas' 1-yard run with only
1:38 left to play. Michigan led 26-22.

The Irish had no plans to go down quietly. They marched to a
third down at the Michigan 30 with only seconds left -- and that's
when Hendricks, a senior strong safety, made his glorious play.

Hendricks started on special teams as a freshman in '96 and
was the starting free safety for the national champions of '97. He
moved to strong safety for his last two seasons.

As Notre Dame hurried to the line of scrimmage, Hendricks
walked over to junior Grady Brooks, an outside linebacker making his first start, and calmly said about their responsibility, "Make
sure you get a jam. Just re-route him and I'll make the play." "I
knew if I did what I had to do, we would be all right," Brooks said.

Notre Dame completed a pass, but Brooks got the jam and
Hendricks tackled the receiver a yard short of the first down. The
Irish couldn't get off another play. As time expired, Hendricks fell

to his knees in tears, overcome by the joy of the moment.

That evening the family gathered for dinner and stories when suddenly a familiar face appeared on TV stopping a Notre Dame receiver. "Hey," Hendricks said. "That's me." Moments later, Hendricks saw himself again; this time he was on his knees in tears as time expired. "Hey, I'm an emotional guy," he said.

And one who had a moment of glory that ESPN highlighted.

You may well remember the play that was your moment of athletic glory. Or the night you received an award from a civic group for your hard work. Your first (and last?) ace on the golf course. Your promotion at work. Your first-ever 10K race. Life does have its moments of glory.

But they all amount to a lesser, transient glory, which actually bears pain with it since you cannot recapture the moment. The excitement, the joy, the happiness – they are fleeting; they pass as quickly as they arose, and you can never experience them again just as Tommy Hendricks can't save the Notre Dame game again.

Glory days that last forever are found only through Jesus. That's because true glory properly belongs only to God, who has shown us his glory in Jesus. To accept Jesus into our lives is thus to take God's glory into ourselves. Glory therefore is an ongoing attribute of Christians. Our glory days are right now, and they will become even more glorious when Jesus returns.

At least I got some highlights on ESPN.
-- Tommy Hendricks after seeing himself on TV in tears

The glory of this earth is fleeting,
but the glory we find in Jesus lasts forever
– and will only get even more magnificent.

DAY 19

RUN FOR IT

Read John 20:1-10.

"Peter and the other disciple started for the tomb. Both were running, but the other disciple outran Peter and reached the tomb first" (vv. 3-4).

Punter Monte Robbins always wanted to run with the ball. He just picked a horrible situation in which to finally give it a try.

From 1984-87, Robbins set almost every one of UM's punting records. He is the career leader in punting average at 42.8 and had three of the four best single season punting averages in Michigan history. Only Zoltan Mesko's 44.5 average in 2009 tops Robbins' three best seasons.

Robbins harbored a secret desire, though, to affect a game with his feet in some way other than kicking. In the 1985 game against Illinois, he saw his chance.

The team was struggling, and Robbins went in on fourth down to punt. He had noticed that an Illinois player charged hard from the left side, and Robbins believed he could blow past him easily and pick up some big yardage. He decided to take off if the player rushed again. The wind also played into his decision. It was blowing right into his face, and he figured he'd hit a lousy punt anyway.

Robbins committed one troubling oversight, though. He failed to check on the distance for the first down; it was 22 yards. "Just a little minor mistake," Robbins called it.

He snared the snap and took off, much to the surprise of everyone, including head coach Bo Schembechler, who had definitely not called for a fake punt given the distance to the down marker. Robbins made the first down, not by much, but he made it.

His daring play fired everyone up, so the players on the sideline were whooping it up when he trotted off the field. His teammates patted him on the back and hugged him as he made his way to his head coach where he knew the real verdict lay.

Schembechler had one quick thing to say: "If you didn't make that first down, I hope you would have known well enough to keep on running."

Hit the ground running -- every morning that's what you do as you leave the house and re-enter the rat race. You run errands; you run though a presentation; you give someone a run for his money; you always want to be in the running and never run-of-the-mill.

You're always running toward something, such as your goals, or away from something, such as your past. Many of us spend much of our lives attempting to run away from God, the purposes he has for us, and the blessings he is waiting to give us.

No matter how hard or how far you run, though, you can never outrun yourself or God. God keeps pace with you, calling you in the short run to take care of the long run by falling to your knees and running for your life -- to Jesus -- just as Peter and the other disciple ran that first Easter morning.

On your knees, you run all the way to glory.

I really wanted to make a play.
> *-- Monte Robbins, explaining his fake punt against Illinois*

You can run to eternity by going to your knees.

DAY 20

TOUGH LOVE

Read Mark 10:17-22.

"'One thing you lack,' [Jesus] said. 'Go, sell everything you have and give to the poor, and you will have treasure in heaven. Then come, follow me.' At this the man's face fell. He went away sad" (vv. 21-22).

Shawn Crable was shocked and angry when head coach Lloyd Carr offered him a set of transfer papers to sign. The linebacker later learned he had been the object of some tough love.

For Crable, football came easy in high school, but everything was different at Michigan. He was injured before he ever played a down in 2003. In 2004, he played sparingly and made only seven tackles. He was optimistic that 2005 would be his breakout year. Thus, when Carr called him to his office prior to the season, Crable showed up anticipating the coach would talk to him about a more active role on the team, maybe even a starting job.

Instead, Carr shoved transfer papers Crable's way and offered to sign them on the spot. Crable had never asked for a transfer and was ambushed by the coach's move. Carr's message was, "You're not going to be successful here because you won't do the things that you told me you would do when I recruited you."

Crable didn't sign the papers, but he was more than a little bit upset when he left the office. He hunted up graduate assistant Sam Sword, a former Wolverine linebacker, to gripe about what Carr had done. He received another surprise. Sword, who ranks third in career tackles for Michigan, told Crable that the head coach had asked him to transfer, too. Carr's brutal honesty was a form of tough love to challenge his underachieving defensive end.

Crable accepted the challenge rather than transferring. In 2006, he was Second-Team All-Big Ten. As a senior in 2007, he was again named to the league's second team. His 28.5 tackles for loss led the Big Ten and was second in the nation.

Tough love helped make a better player out of Shawn Crable.

Do you expect your children to abide by your rules? The recurring reward you receive may be an intense and loud "I hate you," a flounce, and a slammed door. So why do it? Because you're the parent; you love your children, and you want them to become responsible adults. It's tough love.

Jesus also hands out tough love as the story of the young man illustrates. Jesus broke his heart, but the failure was in the young man, who despite his asseverations of devotion, loved his wealth more than he did Jesus.

Jesus is tough on us, too, in that he expects us to follow him no matter what it costs us. A well-executed flounce won't change anything either. As a parent does for his willful children, Jesus knows what is best for us. We'll appreciate that tough love with all our heart and soul on that glorious day when Jesus welcomes us to the place he has prepared for us.

The sterner the discipline, the greater the devotion.
— *Former basketball coach Pete Carril*

**Jesus expects us to do what he has told us to do —
but it's because he loves us and wants the best
for us in life and through eternity.**

YOUNG BLOOD

Read Jeremiah 1:4-10.

*"The Lord said to me, 'Do not say, 'I am only a child'...
for I am with you and will rescue you" (vv. 7a, 8).*

The Wolverines were the new kids on the block, taking on their sport's senior citizen. They didn't give the geezer a lick of respect.

"Maryland Soccer, established 1946." So declared one of the signs that greeted the Michigan men's soccer team on Dec. 4, 2010. The occasion was the match against Maryland in the NCAA quarterfinals for the program's first-ever trip to the College Cup, soccer's equivalent of the Final Four.

That sign pointed out the disparity in the history of the two programs. Michigan coach Steve Burns saw the sign and called it "interesting," noting that the Michigan program had begun as a varsity sport in 2000 after being elevated from club status. That would be more than a half-century after Maryland started its program.

With due deference to their longevity and history, the second-seeded Terrapins, winners of two of the last five national titles, hosted the game against the tenth-seeded Wolverines. "There's an expectation every season at Maryland that we're going to be in the College Cup," admitted the Terrapin head coach.

Apparently nobody bothered to tell those kids from Michigan about those so-called "expectations."

Maryland led 1-0 until four minutes into the last half when

defender Jeff Quijano scored his first goal of the season. Quijano followed that up with a pass to senior forward Justin Meram, who scored to give Michigan its first lead.

The two fought on into a second overtime tied at 2 until the game winner came in the 79th minute. Sophomore midfielder Hamoody Saad hit freshman midfielder Fabio Pereira with a perfect pass, and Pereira scored the winner.

Quite fittingly for an adolescent program, the goal was the first of Pereira's college career.

While our media do seem obsessed with youth, most aspects of our society value experience and some hard-won battle scars. Life usually requires us to spend time on the bench as a reserve, waiting for our chance to play with the big boys and girls. You probably rode some pine in high school. You entered college as a freshman. You started out in your career at an entry-level position.

Paying your dues is traditional, but that should never stop you from doing something bold and daring right away. Nowhere is this more true than in your faith life.

You may assert that you are too young and too inexperienced to really do anything worthwhile for God. Those are just excuses, however, and God won't pay a lick of attention to them when he issues a call.

After all, the younger you are, the more time you have to serve.

You're only young once, but you can be immature forever.
-- Former major leaguer Larry Andersen

Youth is no excuse for not serving God;
it just gives you more time.

DAY 22

REVELATION

Read Isaiah 53.

"But he was pierced for our transgressions, he was crushed for our iniquities; the punishment that brought us peace was upon him, and by his wounds we are healed" (v. 5).

This game is over. We've won this game." It was a ridiculous prediction, made before the Ohio State game began. But the speaker had seen something that led him to make his bold prophecy.

In 1993, the Buckeyes were undefeated, were ranked fifth in the nation, and had already clinched the Big Ten championship. The Wolverines had struggled to a 6-4 record.

The Big Ten office sent the championship trophy to Michigan equipment manager Jon Falk with instructions to get the trophy to the Buckeyes. So the Friday before the game, Falk went to the OSU locker room and tracked down their coaches. He told them how he had wound up with the trophy and left it with them.

As the Buckeyes plodded out of the locker room to practice that afternoon, they stopped to stare at the trophy and to touch it. "They were all talking about the trophy," Falk recalled. "They said things like, 'This is our trophy. We won this trophy.'" Falk said even the coaches held the trophy up to show to the players.

The equipment manager thought all this was clearly odd. He knew that had Gary Moeller or Bo Schembechler seen a similar trophy for their team, they would have told Falk to hide it, declaring "We haven't won anything until we beat Ohio State."

After practice, Falk rushed over to Moeller and made his prediction based on what he had seen in the locker room. Michigan had this game in the bag, he said.

Falk knew of what he spoke. Michigan demolished Ohio State 28-0 with both head coaches expressing their shock at the outcome. Not Jon Falk, though.

In our jaded age, we have pretty much relegated prophecy to dark rooms in which mysterious women peer into crystal balls or clasp our sweaty palms while uttering some vague generalities. At best, we understand a prophet as someone who predicts future events as Jon Falk did.

Within the pages of the Bible, though, we encounter something radically different. A prophet is a messenger from God, one who relays divine revelation to others.

Prophets seem somewhat foreign to us because in one very real sense the age of prophecy is over. In the name of Jesus, we have access to God through our prayers and through scripture. In searching for God's will for our lives, we seek divine revelation. We may speak only for ourselves and not for the greater body of Christ, but we do not need a prophet to discern what God would have us do. We need faith in the one whose birth, life, and death fulfilled more than 300 Bible prophecies.

I gave up a long time ago trying to predict the future and trying to deal with things I couldn't deal with.

-- Brett Favre

**Persons of faith continuously seek
a word from God for their lives.**

DAY 23

YOU DECIDE

Read John 6:60-69.

"The words I have spoken to you are spirit and they are life. Yet there are some of you who do not believe" (vv. 63b-64a).

Mike Trgovac had made a decision. He was just too scared to tell anybody about it.

Trgovac grew up in Ohio as a big Buckeye fan. When he was a senior in high school, Woody Hayes came calling, so his future seemed set. Everything changed, though, when he went to Ann Arbor for a game. He met Bo Schembechler for the first time, and "he was exactly what I was looking for in a coach," Trgovac said.

He went to the Michigan-Ohio State game that year, which Michigan won 22-0, as a guest of the Buckeyes. Halfway through the game, he left his mom and dad and walked over to the Michigan sideline and just watched. He thought, "These guys are pretty cool." Mike Trgovac had decided to play for Michigan.

But telling everyone was another matter.

Hayes and his coaches kept after Trgovac, telling him he was an Ohio kid who should play in Ohio. "It was really hard for me to tell him no, [so] I didn't say anything," Trgovac said.

His mother told him that wherever he decided to go, she would knit him an afghan. The next afternoon when Trgovac came home from school, a bunch of scarlet and gray yarn was on the kitchen table. He couldn't even tell his mother what he had decided.

Finally, though, he told his dad. Together they called Ohio State. When a Buckeye coach kept trying to get to Mike, his dad put an end to it by saying, "Look, this kid made his decision and he's going to Michigan." "I knew for a month where I wanted to go to school," Trgovac said. "I was just really afraid to say it."

At Michigan from 1977-80, Trgovac was a three-year starter at middle guard. He was a two-time All-Big Ten player, was a second team All-America his senior season, and became an NFL coach.

As with Mike Trgovac, the decisions you have made along the way have shaped your life at every pivotal moment. Some decisions you made suddenly and carelessly; some you made carefully and deliberately; some were forced upon you. You may have discovered that some of those spur-of-the-moment decisions have turned out better than your carefully considered ones.

Of all your life's decisions, however, none is more important than one you cannot ignore: What have you done with Jesus? Even in his time, people chose to follow Jesus or to reject him, and nothing has changed; the decision must still be made and nobody can make it for you. Ignoring Jesus won't work either; that is, in fact, a decision, and neither he nor the consequences of your decision will go away.

Carefully considered or spontaneous – how you arrive at a decision for Jesus doesn't matter; all that matters is that you get there.

When I have decisions to make, I find myself thinking about how Bo [Schembechler] would handle this or do that.
-- Mike Trgovac on being a football coach

A decision for Jesus may be spontaneous or considered; what counts is that you make it.

DAY 24

A RIPE OLD AGE

Read Psalm 92.

*"[The righteous] will still bear fruit in old age, they will
stay fresh and green, proclaiming, 'The Lord is upright'"*
(vv. 14-15).

When he played at Michigan, Alvin Wistert was thirteen years
older than some of his teammates.

Alvin was the third Wistert brother to play at Michigan, and the
third Wistert to earn All-American honors. His road to Michigan,
though, was a long, roundabout one.

His first detour came when he dropped out of high school to
play pro baseball. He wasn't interested in football as a youngster.
"I ate, slept, and dreamt baseball," he said. When Michigan's head
baseball coach told him he was better than his brother, Francis,
who had played for Michigan, Alvin decided that his future lay
with baseball.

So he signed a contract with the Cincinnati Reds when he was
17 and left school. His baseball career ended, however, before it
began. In the spring of 1935, he slipped on some ice and landed
hard on his right hand. Enough damage was done that Wistert
could never pitch again.

He left athletics completely, making a living as a salesman for a
while before joining the U.S. Marine Corps. Wistert saw action at
Guam during World War II. While he was in the Corps, he began
to speak of finishing high school and getting to Michigan as had

his brothers, Francis and Albert (See Devotion No. 75.), though he had no background in football.

When the war ended, Wistert was still determined to follow in his brothers' footsteps. He spent a year at Boston University and then arrived in Ann Arbor in 1947. He was 31 years old. Getting into a routine of studying turned out to be harder than the football.

He earned a starting berth at defensive end in '47, the oldest player in Michigan football history. The old man of college football then earned All-American honors in both 1948 and '49. He eventually was inducted into the College Football Hall of Fame.

Thirty-one is rather old for a college football player, especially in our youth-obsessed culture in which we never like to admit that we aren't as young as we used to be.

So we keep plastic surgeons in business, dye our hair, buy cases of those miracle wrinkle-reducing creams, and redouble our efforts in the gym. Sometimes, though, we just have to face up to the truth the mirror tells us: We're getting older every day.

It's really all right, though, because aging and old age are part of the natural cycle of our lives, which was God's idea in the first place. God's conception of the golden years, though, doesn't include unlimited close encounters with a rocking chair and nothing more. God expects us to serve him as we are able all the days of our life. Those who serve God flourish no matter their age because the energizing power of God is in them.

Here comes Pappy and his kids again.
-- Opponents on old-timer Alvin Wistert and his younger teammates

Servants of God don't ever retire; they keep working until they get the ultimate promotion.

DAY 25

THE PRIZE

Read Philippians 3:10-16.

*"I press on toward the goal to win the prize for which God
has called me heavenward in Christ Jesus" (v. 14).*

When Charles Woodson committed to Michigan as a defensive
player, he gave up his dream of winning the Heisman Trophy --
or so he thought. His mother knew better.

"That dream kind of left," was the way Woodson put it about
his childhood hopes for a Heisman. After all, defensive players
didn't win college football's top prize.

Woodson wasn't any ordinary defensive player, though. After
the cornerback's rookie season of 1995 in which he was named
the Big Ten Freshman of the Year, head coach Lloyd Carr asked
Woodson if he'd like to play some tailback. Woodson offered up
a counterproposal: "How about wide receiver?" Thus was born
a two-way player, a throwback to the time before the changes in
the rules in 1965 effectively killed single-platoon football.

And so it was that in the magical 1997 season of the national
championship, Woodson played both ways. He pretty much
clinched the Heisman against Ohio State. With the whole nation
watching, he set up one touchdown with a pass reception, scored
another on a punt return, and stopped a third with an interception.
Woodson "had taken over the game of the year." That afternoon,
"all across America you could practically hear the Heisman ballots
being switched" from Peyton Manning to Woodson.

WOLVERINES

On Dec. 13 the defensive player who had given up his dream won the Heisman Trophy. He was shocked by the announcement, but his mother wasn't. During the Ohio State game, she had asked God for a sign that he would win the trophy. "Just then he made the punt return," she said. "That was the sign He gave me."

"This is sports history," said All-Big Ten safety Marcus Ray, who was Woodson's closest friend on the team. It was history indeed with Woodson joining Tom Harmon and Desmond Howard to become Michigan's third Heisman winner.

Even the most modest and self-effacing among us can't help but be pleased by prizes and honors. They symbolize the approval and appreciation of others, whether it's an All-American team, an Employee of the Month trophy, a plaque for sales achievement, or the sign declaring yours as the neighborhood's prettiest yard.

Such prizes and awards are often the culmination of the pursuit of personal achievement and accomplishment. They represent accolades and recognition from the world. Nothing is inherently wrong with any of that as long as we keep them in perspective.

That is, we must never let awards become such idols that we worship or lower our sight from the greatest prize of all and the only one truly worth winning. It's one that won't rust, collect dust, or leave us wondering why we worked so hard to win it in the first place. The ultimate prize is eternal life, and it's ours through Jesus Christ.

Marcus, I'm going to win every award in God's power.
-- Charles Woodson to his friend Marcus Ray before the '97 season

**God has the greatest prize of all ready
to hand to you through Jesus Christ.**

DAY 26

THE SUB

Read Galatians 3:10-14.

"Christ redeemed us from the curse of the law by becoming a curse for us" (v. 13).

Never before or since has there been a substitute quite like Steve Fisher, who won a national championship while he was the "interim" coach; i.e, a sub for the real thing.

On the eve of the 1989 NCAA Tournament, Michigan athletic director Bo Schembechler fired basketball head coach Bill Frieder, who had agreed to become Arizona State's head coach at season's end. "A Michigan man will coach Michigan, not an Arizona State man," a miffed Schembechler declared.

Only the night before the firing, Frieder had told his assistants about his decision. While he was surprised, Fisher, a nine-year assistant, couldn't help but speculate about what would happen. "I didn't know if they'd let him coach the team or if they'd be upset with him. I wouldn't have been surprised either way," he said.

Thus, Fisher wasn't totally dumbfounded when Schembechler summoned him to his office at 7:30 the next morning and named him the interim coach -- but just for the NCAA Tournament. His job was to step in for the real head coach and ensure that the team at least made a decent showing in the tournament.

Instead, Fisher became the ultimate sub and the Wolverines became the story of the whole season, "college basketball's improbable princes." Though shocked by the change, the players were apparently quite comfortable with the familiar face and voice that Fisher presented. With their substitute head coach, they went on an improbable six-game run to win the national title. In one of the most exciting championship games in history, junior point guard Rumeal Robinson hit a pair of free throws with three seconds left in overtime to beat Seton Hall 80-79.

The ultimate sub was named the Michigan head coach a week after the tournament and stayed on the job until 1997.

Wouldn't it be cool if you had a substitute like Steve Fisher for all of life's hard stuff? Telling of a death in the family? Call in your sub. Breaking up with your boyfriend? Job interview? Chemistry test? Crucial presentation at work? Let the sub handle it.

We do have such a substitute, but not for the matters of life. Instead, Jesus is our substitute for matters of life and death. Since Jesus has already made it, we don't have to make the sacrifice God demands for forgiveness and salvation.

One of the ironies of our age is that many people desperately grope for a substitute for Jesus. Mysticism, human philosophies such as Scientology, false religions such as Hinduism and Islam, cults, New Age approaches that preach self-fulfillment without responsibility or accountability – they and others like them are all pitiful, inadequate substitutes for Jesus.

Accept no substitutes. It's Jesus or nothing.

Maybe I ought to retire right now. Steve Fisher is unbeaten, untied and the happiest man alive.
-- Steve Fisher after the '89 NCAA Tournament

**There is no substitute for Jesus,
the consummate substitute.**

THE NIGHTMARE

Read Mark 5:1-20.

"What do you want with me, Jesus, Son of the Most High God? Swear to God that you won't torture me!" (v. 7)

Lloyd Carr called the play "the greatest nightmare I've ever experienced in sports," and for a few sickening seconds, he feared he was about to endure it again.

On Sept. 24, 1994, on the last play of the game, Colorado's quarterback "heaved a tight spiral 73 yards into the gathering darkness of an Ann Arbor evening." Knowing that it was coming, the Wolverines had the Hail Mary defensed, but they couldn't cover luck. The deflected ball wound up in the arms of a Buffalo receiver, who fell into the end zone for a 27-26 Colorado win.

For two years, until the teams played again on Sept. 14, 1996, the Michigan nightmare that was that play would not go away. Carr was the defensive coordinator under Gary Moeller for that '94 game. He was the Wolverine head coach in '96, and he decided months before the rematch he would not talk about the nightmare.

But here it was, raising itself up again, with only five seconds left in the '96 game and Michigan leading 20-13. With the ball on the Wolverine 37, Colorado's quarterback dropped back and looked at four receivers sprinting for the end zone. "I was sick," Carr later admitted as he watched the flight of that last-gasp pass just as he had watched helplessly two years before.

As in 1994, the Wolverines had this game won, but the UM

quarterback bobbled the snap and lost the chance to run out the clock. Colorado had five seconds for a shot at another nightmare.

Michigan's defense rumbled onto the field, knowing what was coming. "Nobody said anything about two years ago," said sophomore cornerback Charles Woodson, "but you knew everybody was thinking about it." Nose tackle Will Carr admitted as much, saying, "I thought, here we go again." So did Lloyd Carr.

But Michigan senior safety Chuck Winters knocked the ball to the ground, ending the two-year nightmare.

Falling. Drowning. Standing naked in a room crowded with fully dressed people. They're nightmares, dreams that jolt us from our sleep in anxiety or downright terror. The film industry has used our common nightmares to create horror movies that allow us to experience our fears vicariously. This includes the formulaic "evil vs. good" movies in which demons and the like render good virtually helpless in the face of their power and ruthlessness.

The spiritual truth, though, is that it is evil that has come face to face with its worst nightmare in Jesus. We seem to understand that our basic mission as Jesus' followers is to further his kingdom and change the world through emulating him in the way we live and love others. But do we appreciate that in truly living for Jesus, we are daily tormenting the very devil himself?

Satan and his lackeys quake helplessly in fear before the power of almighty God that is in us through Jesus.

We've suffered enough because of that play.
-- Lloyd Carr on the '94 Colorado nightmare

**As the followers of Jesus Christ,
we are the stuff of Satan's nightmares.**

DAY 28

IMPOSSIBLE DREAM

Read Matthew 19:16-26.

"Jesus looked at them and said, 'With man this is impossible, but with God all things are possible'" (v. 26).

On Sept. 4, 2010, in front of the largest crowd in college football history, Elliott Mealer's brother, Brock, did what the doctors had said was impossible. He walked.

Elliott Mealer thought God was joking. A big Ohio State fan, the big offensive lineman had prayed, asking God where he wanted him to play his college football. God's answer came in the form of a series of signs that pointed -- of all places -- to Ann Arbor. So Elliott committed to Michigan.

Then on Christmas Eve 2007, an elderly driver broadsided his family's vehicle. He escaped relatively unscathed, but his father and his girlfriend were killed. His brother, Brock, suffered two shattered vertebrae. The doctors were unanimous in their prognosis: Walking again was impossible. Life in a wheelchair "is the best I could hope for," Brock recalled. "They always wanted me to accept that fact."

In October 2009, Elliott was a redshirt freshman guard at Michigan. At the time, Brock's physical therapy occasionally brought him to Ann Arbor for workouts designed by UM strength and conditioning director Mike Barwis. During one of those workouts, Barwis asked Brock a simple but startling question: Was he ready to get out of that wheelchair?

WOLVERINES

Thus began what for Brock Mealer was an impossible journey.

Barwis created a plan specifically for Brock. He worked out four days a week in the Wolverine football weight room, often wearing a navy blue T-shirt that read, "Impossible Is Nothing."

On Sept. 4, 2010, Brock Mealer led the Wolverines onto the field for the season opener against the UConn Huskies. Then, assisted by a pair of canes and surrounded by his brothers and his mother, he got out of his wheelchair and walked to midfield.

Brock Mealer had become the living embodiment for the UM football team of what is possible.

Let's face it. Any pragmatic person, no matter how deep his faith, has to admit that God's children have succeeded in turning his beautiful little world into an impossible mess. The only hope for this dying, sin-infested place lies in our Lord's return to set everything right.

But we can't just sit around all day doing nothing but praying for Jesus' return, as glorious a day as that will be. Our mission in this world is to change it for Jesus. We serve a Lord who calls us to step out in faith into seemingly impossible situations. We serve a Lord so audacious that he inspires us to believe that we are the instruments through which God does the impossible.

Changing the world may indeed seem impossible. Changing our corner of it, however, is not. It is, rather, a very possible, doable act of faith.

It's up to God and Brock to make it work, and I have faith in both.
-- Mike Barwis on his plan to get Brock Mealer back on his feet

With God, nothing is impossible,
including changing the world for Jesus.

DAY 29

JINXED

Read Jonah 1.

"Tell us, who is responsible for making all this trouble for us? What did you do?" (v. 8a)

The jinx appeared to be alive and well -- until the fourth quarter.

As Michigan prepared to take on Michigan State in East Lansing on Oct. 10, 1964, the Wolverines had lost to the Spartans with such regularity that the press openly wrote of a jinx. Michigan had not beaten State in nine tries, managing only two ties, and had won only twice in the last thirteen seasons.

State scored early, and that lone touchdown held up deep into the fourth quarter with the Spartans leading 10-3. But Michigan's offense suddenly came alive. Quarterback Bob Timberlake, who would be first-team All-America and the Big Ten Player of the Year, hit end John Henderson with a 29-yard pass to the State 21. Three plays later, Timberlake found sophomore halfback Rick Sygar with a five-yard swing pass for a score. With just under seven minutes to play, the Wolverines were within a single point.

Michigan coach Bump Elliott decided to go for two because "we wanted to win it right here and then." The largest crowd in stadium history to that point watched "in a single, held breath" as Timberlake rolled out and pitched to fullback Mel Anthony. The Spartan defense was ready, stopping him just short of the goal.

The jinx had held.

But All-American tackle Bill Yearby led a defensive stand that forced an MSU punt. Dick Rindfuss returned the kick to the State 41. The Wolverines turned to smash-mouth football, and three running plays moved the ball to a first down at the 31.

Those runs set up the game-winning play. With only 2:33 left, Timberlake pitched to Sygar, who stopped and lofted a pass to Henderson, who was wide open. He scored easily, and Timberlake then passed to end Steve Smith for the two-point conversion.

The 17-10 win ended forever any talk of a Michigan State jinx.

Usually when one team consistently beats another, it has more to do with coaching and talent than any superstitious drivel.

Some people do feel, however, that they exist under a dark and rainy cloud. Nothing goes right; all their dreams collapse around them; they seem to constantly bring about misery on themselves and also on the ones around them.

Why? Is it really a hex, a jinx?

Nonsense. The Bible provides us an excellent example in Jonah of a person who those around him – namely the sailors on the boat with him -- believed to be a hex. Jonah's life was a mess, but it had nothing to do with a jinx. His life was in shambles because he was disobeying God.

Take a careful look at people you know whose lives are in shambles, including some who profess to believe in God. The key to life lies not just in believing; the responsibility of the believer is to obey God. Problems lie not in hexes but in disobedience.

It just feels real good.
-- UM head coach Bump Elliott on ending the so-called jinx

Hexes don't cause us trouble,
but disobedience to God sure does.

GOD'S CONQUERORS

Read John 16:19-33.

"In this world you will have trouble. But take heart! I have overcome the world" (v. 33b).

The parents hoped their son would gravitate toward soccer seeing as how he was born without any fingers on his right hand. But Jim Abbott loved baseball; not only that, he wanted to pitch.

Abbott's story, of course, is the stuff of legend. He pitched with his glove resting on his fingerless right hand. Once he released the ball, he slipped his left hand into the glove. He would then field a ball, stick the glove under his right arm, let the ball fall into his left hand, and throw to the base. The nifty legerdemain became known as the Abbott switch.

He pitched a no-hitter in his first Little League start when he was 11. When he was a freshman in high school, a coach ordered eight straight hitters to bunt on him. The first batter reached base safely; Abbott threw the next seven out.

Michigan baseball coach Bud Middaugh was skeptical about a one-handed pitcher. "I just hoped he'd be a competent college pitcher," he admitted. "He turned out far better than I imagined."

Indeed he did. Abbott completed his Michigan career in 1988 with an overall record of 26-8 record and a career 3.03 ERA. He was named Big Ten Player of the Year and Big Ten Male Athlete of the Year. In 2009, the university retired his uniform number 31; he was the first player in the program's history to be so honored.

WOLVERINES

Abbott went on to a ten-year career in the major leagues that included throwing a no-hitter at the New York Yankees in 1993.

"I don't ever remember it being something I had to master," Abbott once said about pitching despite the difficulties presented by his right hand. "It was just something I did."

It was just something he overcame.

We each have a choice to make about how we live. We can just survive or we can overcome as Jim Abbott did.

We often hear inspiring stories of people who triumph by overcoming especially daunting obstacles. Those barriers may be physical or mental disabilities or great personal tragedies or injustice. When we hear of them, we may well respond with a little prayer of thanksgiving that life has been kinder to us.

But all people of faith, no matter how drastic the obstacles they face, must ultimately overcome the same opponent: the Satan-infested world. Some do have it tougher than others, but we all must fight daily to remain confident and optimistic.

To merely survive from day to day is to give up by surrendering our trust in God's involvement in our daily life. To overcome, however, is to stand up to the world and fight its temptations that would erode the armor of our faith in Jesus Christ.

Today is a day for you to overcome by remaining faithful. The very hosts of Heaven wait to hail the conquering hero.

I want to be remembered not for having to overcome anything, but for making the most of what God gave me.

-- *Jim Abbott*

Life's difficulties provide us a chance to experience the true joy of victory in Jesus.

DAY 31

CONFIDENCE MAN

Read Micah 7:5-7.

"As for me, I will look to the Lord, I will wait for the God of my salvation" (v. 7 NRSV).

The freshman wide receiver had so much confidence that with time running out he told his quarterback to throw him the ball. The result was one of the greatest plays in Big House history.

Michigan's 1979 homecoming was turning out to be anything but a joyous reunion. With only six seconds on the clock, the 6-1 Wolverines were facing a 21-21 tie with a scrappy band of Indiana Hoosiers. Fullback Lawrence Reid had caught a pass and flung the ball out of bounds at the Indiana 45 to stop the clock.

The Wolverines huddled to call their last play, and that's when the confident freshman piped up. He told quarterback John Wangler, "Wangs, you throw that ball to ME!" Senior wingback Ralph Clayton give the kid a look that said what everybody must have been thinking: What is this freshman talking about?

This was no ordinary freshman, though. It was Anthony Carter. A three-time All-America, Carter finished at Ann Arbor as the school's all-time leading receiver. He set receiving records for touchdowns, receptions, and receiving yards, among others. He still holds the NCAA career record for highest average gain per play. He was the Big Ten MVP in 1982 and was inducted into the College Football Hall of Fame in 2001.

Against Indiana that homecoming day, though, he was just an

WOLVERINES

untested freshman who caught more than two passes in a game only once that season. But he was confident, and Wangler saw it. He told Carter he would get the ball to him.

He did, hitting the freshman in front of the Indiana defensive backs, who were playing a deep zone coverage. A tackler knocked him off balance, but he put his hand on his ground, recovered, and then took off. He avoided one defender "and danced into the end zone with his arms raised" with no time left on the clock.

Having confidently demanded the ball, Carter turned in a play that has become a truly legendary moment for Wolverine fans.

You need confidence in all areas of your life. You're confident the company you work for will pay you on time, or you wouldn't go to work. You turn the ignition confident your car will start. When you flip a switch, you expect the light to come on.

Confidence in other people and in things is often misplaced, though. Companies go broke; car batteries die; light bulbs burn out. Even the people you love the most sometimes let you down.

So where can you place your trust with absolute confidence you won't be betrayed? In the promises of God.

Such confidence is easy, of course, when everything's going your way, but what about when you cry as Micah did, "What misery is mine!" As Micah declares, that's when your confidence in God must be its strongest. That's when you wait for the Lord confident that God will not fail you and will never let you down.

I just had the confidence that I could make something happen.
-- Anthony Carter on the legendary play vs. Indiana

People, things, and organizations will let you down; only God can be trusted confidently.

DAY 32

AS A RULE

Read Luke 5:27-32.

"Why do you eat and drink with tax collectors and 'sinners'?" (v. 30b)

Yale Van Dyne received a life-changing message about abiding by life's rules from -- of all things -- a fortune cookie.

In high school, Van Dyne sent letters to the schools he wanted to play for, and when Bo Schembechler wrote back, he decided to walk on. He arrived in Ann Arbor in 1987.

For a walk-on, Van Dyne did all right. He made the team and lettered three times. As a junior wide receiver in 1990, he caught eleven passes for 126 yards; his senior season he had 39 receptions for 500 yards and two touchdowns. Playing for Schembechler and Gary Moeller, he was a part of four conference champions and made three trips to the Rose Bowl.

Van Dyne didn't start out as the greatest student at Michigan, however. With his trait of assigning players whatever names he wanted to, Schembechler always called Van Dyne "Harvard Van Dyne." After Van Dyne's first-semester grades were released, the head coach told him if he didn't get a 3.0 average the next semester, "I'm going to stop calling you Harvard and start calling you Washtenaw Community College."

When Van Dyne was lackadaisical in his class attendance, his position coach, Cam Cameron, kicked him off the team. "I'm going to give you a life lesson by dismissing you," the coach said.

WOLVERINES

"You're not doing the small things to succeed."

That sent Van Dyne to a local Chinese restaurant with his girl friend to carry on through dinner about how unfair his dismissal was. After the meal, he opened a fortune cookie; it read, "Those who don't play by the rules shouldn't complain."

Right then and there, Van Dyne realized what was wrong with his life. He was allowed back onto the team and went from there.

You live by rules that others set up. Some lender determined the interest rate on your mortgage and your car loan. You work hours and shifts somebody else established. Someone else decided what day your garbage gets picked up and what school district your house is in.

Jesus encountered societal rules also, including a strict set of religious edicts that dictated what company he should keep, what people, in other words, were fit for him to socialize with, talk to, or share a meal with. Jesus ignored the rules, choosing love instead of mindless obedience and demonstrating his disdain for society's rules by mingling with the outcasts, the lowlifes, the poor, and the misfits.

You, too, have to choose when you find yourself in the presence of someone whom society deems undesirable. Will you choose the rules or love? Are you willing to be a rebel for love — as Jesus was for you?

You're not getting the basic tenets of being successful in life.
-- Coach Cam Cameron to Yale Van Dyne on living by the rules

Society's rules dictate who is acceptable
and who is not, but love in the name of Jesus
knows no such distinctions.

DAY 33

THE REWARD

Read 1 Corinthians 3:10-17.

"If what he has built survives, he will receive his reward"
(v. 14).

The only reward Max Pollock expected was to come out alive.
He wound up getting much more than that.

"I think my goal originally was to stick it out the four years
and just survive Michigan football." Spoken like the true walk-on
Pollock was.

In high school, Pollock was recruited by Ivy League and other
East Coast colleges, but an aunt and uncle had inundated him
with all things Michigan at an early age. So in the fall of 2004, he
passed up what offers he had and walked on at Michigan.

Not surprisingly, since no one knew anything about him as a
football player, Pollock was "buried under everybody else on the
depth chart. At first, it seems like an exercise in futility," he said.
"You're really not making any progress."

But he was on the team, which is the only reward a walk-on
can realistically expect. In his first two seasons, the linebacker
got into three games during garbage time. But in the 2006 game
against Central Michigan, everything changed.

With Michigan coasting 34-10, "the coaches decided to give the
hard-working walk-on some reps in front of the Big House crowd."
What happened was an inspiration for walk-ons everywhere.

Pollock dropped back into coverage on a pass play and made a fingertip interception "that would have made any wide receivers' coach proud." But there was more. He had 12 yards of nothing but grass in front of him. Max Pollock scored a touchdown.

That wasn't his only reward. Pollock eventually earned a scholarship. He lettered in 2006 and '07. His senior season he played in eleven games and had three tackles.

Pollock also received a reward that was even greater than all those things. As head coach Lloyd Carr put it, Pollock "gained the respect of every man in our program."

We want our rewards now. Hire a new football coach; he better win right away. You want to keep me happy? Then let's see a raise and a promotion immediately or I'm looking for another job. Want that new car or big house you can't afford? Hey that's what they make credit for, so I can live the good life without having to wait.

Jesus spoke often about rewards, but in terms of eternal salvation and service to others rather than instant gratification or self-aggrandizement. The reward Jesus has in mind for us is the inevitable result of the way of life Jesus taught. To live with faith in God and in service to others is to move surely – if not swiftly – toward the eternal rewards included in our salvation.

The world's ephemeral material rewards may pass us by if we don't grab them right now. God's eternal spiritual rewards, however, will absolutely be ours.

You can look at the touchdown as a reward, but I still have all these goals. I want to start playing more.
-- Max Pollock after the Central Michigan game

**God rewards our faith, patience, and service
by fulfilling the promises he has made to us.**

THE PIONEER SPIRIT

Read Luke 5:1-11.

*"So they pulled their boats up on shore, left everything
and followed him" (v. 11).*

They were a mostly longhaired and scruffy bunch" who didn't
look much like pioneers. But they were.

On Feb. 12, 2012, the Michigan men's lacrosse team took on the
University of Detroit in Pontiac. In itself, there was little remarkable about that. The university has had a men's lacrosse team in
some fashion since 1965. The program actually began in 1940 but
was discontinued with the onset of World War II. What made this
day special was that it marked the official debut of men's lacrosse
at Michigan as a varsity sport.

In May 2011, UM director of athletics Dave Brandon announced
that the men's and women's lacrosse teams would be elevated
from club status to varsity status with the men starting play in
2012 and the women a year later.

For the men, the move represented a major step up in the cali-
ber of the competition. Under head coach John Paul for fourteen
seasons, the team had a 241-44 record and had won the club level
national title eleven of the past thirteen seasons.

All that was behind them, though, on that cold February day.
In that first-ever game, Paul started four seniors as a reward for
their pioneer spirit: Brian Greiner, Austin Swaney, Robert Healy,
and Trevor Yealy. This whole team of trailblazers was the bunch

WOLVERINES

one writer said didn't look like the stereotype of a jock. They were "far from physically imposing or impressive."

Sophomore midfielder Doug Bryant made history five minutes into the first quarter when he scored the first goal in the program's history. The Wolverines lost, though, 13-9.

They did not get their first-ever varsity win until March 4, a 14-4 defeat of the Mercer University Bears. The victory came as a relief to the team. With that milestone behind them, they could get on about the business of building this brand new varsity sport.

Going to a place in your life you've never been before requires a willingness to take risks and face uncertainty head-on. You may have never helped start a new sports program at a major college, but you've had your moments when your latent pioneer spirit manifested itself. That time you changed careers, ran a marathon, volunteered at a homeless shelter, or went back to school.

While attempting new things invariably begets apprehension, the truth is that when life becomes too comfortable and too familiar, it gets boring. The same is true of God, who is downright dangerous because he calls us to be anything but comfortable as we serve him. He summons us to continuously blaze new trails in our faith life, to follow him no matter what. Stepping out on faith is risky all right, but the reward is a life of accomplishment, adventure, and joy that cannot be equaled anywhere else.

I will never forget this game -- though it wasn't the outcome we wanted.
-- Trevor Yealy on UM's first varsity lacrosse game

Unsafe and downright dangerous, God calls us out of the place where we are comfortable to a life of adventure and trailblazing in his name.

DAY 35

QUIET TIME

1 Kings 19:1-13.

"And after the earthquake a fire, but the Lord was not in the fire: and after the fire a still small voice" (v. 12 KJV).

The quiet was downright eerie -- except, of course, to the Wolverines, who had caused it in the first place.

As usual, in 1976, the Big Ten championship and the Rose-Bowl berth were on the line when the Wolverines traveled to Columbus to take on the Buckeyes on Nov. 20. Once-defeated Michigan was ranked second; once-defeated Ohio State was ranked eighth. "It was probably, to this day, out of all the games I've ever played in, the hardest fought and hardest-hitting game I've ever played in, and that includes my career in the NFL," said two-time All-Big Ten offensive lineman Mike Kenn.

The game was scoreless at halftime, but on their first possession of the last half, the Wolverines drove and scored. Ohio State punted and Michigan scored. Ohio State punted and Michigan scored. It was 22-0. Ohio State punted and Michigan was driving again -- when suddenly with about six minutes left to play, head coach Bo Schembechler called a time out.

Along with the rest of the offense, Kenn was surprised and confused by the call. He trotted to the sideline where Schembechler bellowed, "First offense, you're done for the day." So the second team went in, and the first teamers went to the bench at the 50-yard line -- where they realized what their coach had done. He

WOLVERINES

had given them the chance to enjoy what they had accomplished: dominating their most bitter rival on their home turf.

That's when Kenn first noticed the silence. "All of a sudden I realized, it was dead quiet," he said. He looked across the field and saw a silent and scowling Woody Hayes. No player or coach was within ten yards of him.

"It was the greatest game I ever played in my life," Kenn said, but he always remembered that strange, eerie quiet.

The television blares; the ring tone sounds off; the dishwasher rattles. Outside, the roar of traffic assaults your ears; a siren screams until you wince; the garbage collectors bang and slam the cans around; and everybody shouts to be heard above the din.

We live in a noisy world. Strangely enough, the most powerful voice of all – the one whose voice spoke the universe into being -- does not join in the cacophony. We would expect Almighty God to speak in a thunderous roar, complete with lightning, that forces us to cover our ears and fall to our knees in dread.

Instead, God patiently waits for us to turn to him, nudging us gently with a still small voice. Thus, in the serenity of quiet time expressly set aside for God, and not in the daily tumult, do we find God and discover something rather remarkable: that God's being with us is not remarkable at all. He's always there; we just can't hear him most of the time over the world's noise.

There were 87,000 people in that stadium, and you couldn't hear a word.
-- Mike Kenn on the '76 Ohio State game

God speaks in a whisper, not a shout,
so we must listen carefully,
or we will miss his voice altogether.

DAY 36

GIFT-WRAPPED

Read James 1:13-18.

"Every good and perfect gift is from above, coming down from the Father of the heavenly lights" (v. 17).

When Dave Molk scored the only touchdown of his football life, he ran over to his mother and gave the ball to her. It was the last time she saw him play.

In 2011, Molk, a senior and four-year letterman, won the Rimington Trophy as the best center in college football. He was a consensus first-team All-America and first-team All-Big Ten.

Molk is the rare individual who was drawn to football because of the weight room. "Dave Molk is the one guy in the history of all official visits to request to go straight to the weight room on his visit to lift," said UM defensive end Ryan Van Bergen, Molk's roommate. "How meat-headed is that?"

That passion in the weight room spilled over onto the field. Before every Michigan game for four seasons, Molk greeted one of his fellow offensive linemen with a head butt. His victim for 2011 was freshman Jack Miller, who said he didn't mind the assault too much as long as he knew it was coming.

That tenacity on the sideline and on the field meant Molk was on his third helmet by the Minnesota game, the fifth game of the 2011 season. He had cracked the first two.

Molk's size was a gift from his dad, who was 6-foot-5. His heart was a gift from his mother, whom he called "the toughest person I've ever met."

She battled breast cancer for 12 years, but during the fall Dave was 12, it spread to her brain. She was at the field that day the coach moved Dave from the line to tailback and called his number at the goal line. When he scored, he picked himself up and took off running, through a gate and up a hill. He handed the football to his mother and said, "This is for you, Mom."

A month later, she died at home with her family and that football there in the room with her.

Receiving a gift is nice, but giving has its pleasures too, doesn't it? The children's excitement on Christmas morning. That smile of pure delight on your spouse's face when you came up with a really cool anniversary present. Your dad's surprise that time you didn't give him a tie or socks. There really does seem to be something to this being more blessed to give than to receive.

No matter how generous we may be, though, we are grumbling misers compared to God, the greatest gift-giver of all. That's because all the good things in our lives – every one of them – come from God. Friends, love, health, family, the air we breathe, the sun that warms us, even our very lives are all gifts from a profligate God. And here's the kicker: He even gives us eternal life with him through the gift of his son.

What in the world can we possibly give God in return? Our love and our life.

She showed me just how precious life is.
– Dave Molk on one of the gifts he got from his mother

No one can match God as a giver, but you can give him the gift of your love in appreciation.

DAY 37

PAYBACK

Read Matthew 5:38-42.

"I tell you, Do not resist an evil person. If someone strikes you on the right cheek, turn to him the other also" (v. 39).

Michigan's rookie head coach believed his Wolverines could exact revenge on the Buckeyes, but he was clearly in the minority.

In 1968, Ohio State "steamrolled the Wolverines on their way to a national championship." Michigan changed coaches; the Buckeyes got better. In November of '69, they were ranked No. 1 and "were being hailed as perhaps the greatest team in college football history. They were a juggernaut."

Amidst all that hoopla, few folks seemed to notice that the new guy in Ann Arbor, Bo Schembechler, was doing a pretty good job. Michigan was 7-2 and were ranked 12th in the country. Still, the Wolverines were 17-point underdogs for The Game.

Schembechler clearly wanted his players thinking revenge. He had "50-14," the score of the ignominious beatdown of the year before, stenciled on the jerseys of the scout team during practice. "Ohio State is beatable," he told the press.

Despite the consensus that the game would be one-sided, the largest crowd in college football history jammed the stadium. From the first series, "it looked like something magical might actually be flitting about in the crisp November air."

The Wolverines led 14-12 when Barry Pierson returned a punt 60 yards to the OSU 3 "in one of the biggest runs in Michigan football history." Quarterback Don Moorehead scored two plays later to make it a two-score lead. The 24-12 halftime score was the final. In what Schembechler called "one of the greatest performances I have ever seen," Pierson intercepted three passes in the last half as the defense completely shut Ohio State down.

With the clock ticking to zero, jubilant fans chanted "Good-bye, Woody" and "We're No. 1." They, too, enjoyed payback time.

The very nature of an intense rivalry such as Michigan and Ohio State is that the loser will seek payback for the defeat of the season before. But what about in life when somebody's done you wrong; is it time to get even?

The problem with revenge in real-life is that it isn't as clear-cut as a scoreboard. Life is so messy that any attempt at revenge is often inadequate or, worse, backfires and injures you.

As a result, you remain gripped by resentment and anger, which hurts you and no one else. You poison your own happiness while that other person goes blithely about her business. The only way someone who has hurt you can keep hurting you is if you're a willing participant.

But it doesn't have to be that way. Jesus ushered in a new way of living when he taught that we are not to seek revenge for personal wrongs and injuries. Let it go and go on with your life. What a relief!

The revenge factor gives Michigan every incentive to win.
-- Bo Schembechler on the '69 Ohio State game

Resentment and anger over a wrong injures you,
not the other person, so forget it --
just as Jesus taught.

DAY 38

BLESS YOU

Read Romans 5:1-11.

"We also rejoice in our sufferings because we know that suffering produces perseverance; perseverance, character; and character, hope. And hope does not disappoint us"
(vv. 3-5a).

For Holly Hein, a torn ACL was a blessing in disguise. It may well have saved her life.

When Greg Ryan took over the Michigan women's soccer program prior to the 2008 season, Hein was his first recruit. She made an immediate impact, starting nineteen games as a freshman in 2009. Her sophomore season was waylaid, though, by a torn ACL after six games. During surgery in October 2010 to repair the ACL, an anesthesiologist noticed an abnormal lump on the side of her neck. Hein was unaware of the mass; it had caused her no pain.

Four months later, Hein's neck suddenly swelled up, but the doctors could find no answer. Aware of the mass since the ACL surgery, Hein knew deep down that something was seriously wrong, so she refused to just let it go. Before she returned to Ann Arbor in July 2011, she saw a new set of doctors at her home in California. This time, the doctors performed a biopsy.

Hein was back in Ann Arbor when her doctor called with the stunning news that she had thyroid cancer. Hein used the direct approach to inform her parents and her teammates. "I told them straight out," she said. The reaction of sophomore defender Tori

WOLVERINES

McCombs was typical: "When she got into the middle of the room, we thought, 'she's ready to quit.' Then she dropped that on us."

Hein played six games that fall, as many as she could without losing a year of eligibility. On Sept. 29, 2011, she had surgery. Six days later, she was on the practice field, surprising her teammates. She said she felt great and was plotting her return to the field.

She had plans and hopes because she had the tragedy of a torn ACL that ultimately was a blessing.

We just never know what God is up to. We can know, though, that he's always busy preparing blessings for us and that if we trust and obey him, he will pour out those blessings upon us.

Some of those blessings, however, come disguised as hardship and suffering as was the case with Holly Hein and her torn ACL. That's often true in our own lives, too, and it is only after we can look back upon what we have endured that we understand it as a blessing.

The key lies in trusting God, in realizing that God isn't out to destroy us but instead is interested only in doing good for us, even if that means allowing us to endure the consequences of a difficult lesson. God doesn't manage a candy store; more often, he relates to us as a stern but always loving father.

If we truly love and trust God, no matter what our situation is now, he has blessings in store for us. This, above all, is our greatest hope.

Always have the attitude of gratitude and count your blessings.
-- Former NFL head coach Tony Dungy

Life's hardships are often transformed into blessings when we endure them trusting in God.

DAY 39

SEEING THE VISION

Read Acts 26:1, 9-23.

"So then, . . . I was not disobedient to the vision from heaven" (v. 19).

Fielding H. Yost was such a visionary that the evidence of his vision for Michigan athletics is all over the campus today.

Athletic director Charles Baird hired Yost as the head football coach in 1901 for a professor's pay, $2,300 a year, and room and board. Everything about athletics at Michigan changed from the day the 30-year-old ran from the train station to campus.

He arrived determined to move the Wolverines to the center of the national football stage. To that end, he scheduled intersectional games. When the Big Ten limited the number of outside games his teams could play, Yost responded by pulling out of the conference. He returned in 1917 when it suited his purposes.

The vision morphed into reality immediately. The Wolverines weren't just the champions of the West but national champions in Yost's first four seasons in Ann Arbor.

Over 25 seasons, Yost won more than 83 percent of his games, six national titles, and ten conference titles. He also won the first-ever Rose Bowl, which nearly killed the game. The 49-0 win over Stanford in 1901 was so lopsided fourteen years passed before committee members managed the resolve to play a second game.

The most astounding manifestation of Yost's vision is Michigan Stadium. Yost built it in 1927 with a capacity of 84,401. Critics said college football would never generate enough interest to fill it up. He ignored them, instead actually having the vision to install an extra foundation to allow for construction of a second deck.

"I'm interested in fitness for all," Yost once said. So as athletic director, he built the nation's first intramural sports building and the first-ever multipurpose field house, the latter still being used as Yost Ice Arena. He also oversaw construction of a world-class golf course.

Still today, the university reaps the benefits of Yost's vision.

To speak of visions is often to risk their being lumped with palm readings, Ouija boards, seances, horoscopes, and other such useless mumbo-jumbo. The danger such mild amusements pose, however, is very real in that they indicate a reliance on something other than God. It is God who knows the future; it is God who has a vision and a plan for your life; it is God who has the answers you seek as you struggle to find your way.

You probably do have a vision for your life, a plan for how it should unfold. It's the dream you pursue through your family, your job, your hobbies, your interests. But your vision inspires a fruitful life only if it is compatible with God's plan.

As the apostle Paul found out, you ignore God's vision at your peril. But if you pursue it, you'll find an even more glorious life than you could ever have envisioned for yourself.

He had great foresight. He had great imagination.
-- Howard Wikel on his friend, Fielding Yost

Your grandest vision for the future
pales beside the vision God has of what
the two of you can accomplish together.

THE HOMEPLACE

Read Joshua 24:14-27.

"Choose for yourselves this day whom you will serve. . . .
But as for me and my household, we will serve the Lord"
(v. 15).

Michigan Stadium on game day is such a homefield advantage that an opposing quarterback once wet his pants when he saw it.

The first game played in The Big House was a 33-0 whipping of Ohio Wesleyan on Oct. 1, 1927. The structure was built on land so wet that the surface resembled quicksand; it swallowed a crane during construction that still remains under the stadium.

Today, Michigan Stadium is the biggest stadium in the country with an official capacity of 109,901. Since Nov. 8, 1975, every home football game has drawn a crowd of 100,000 or more. In the mid '80s, that impressive sight was just too much for one Wisconsin quarterback to handle.

Fred Jackson joined the Michigan coaching staff in 1992. His stops before Ann Arbor included a stint from 1982-86 at Wisconsin. He was coaching the quarterbacks and receivers at the time, and not long after his players took the field to warm up, the starting quarterback headed toward the tunnel. Jackson asked him where he was headed, and he replied, "I'm sorry, coach. I'll be right back. I just wet my pants."

A startled Jackson said, "What!" The youngster explained that he had never seen this many people together before. "They're yelling and screaming either for you or against you, and I just couldn't hold it."

Jackson knew the Badgers were in trouble. "I thought we had a great chance to win that day," he said, "but when that happened I knew we were in trouble. . . . And actually, the kid went on to play a pretty good game."

The Badgers still lost. The Wolverine talent and that decided homefield advantage were just too much.

You enter your home to find love, security, and joy. It's the place where your heart feels warmest, your laughter comes easiest, and your life is its richest. It is the center of and the reason for everything you do and everything you are.

How can a home be such a place?

If it is a home where grace is spoken before every meal, it is such a place. If it is a home where the Bible is read, studied, and discussed by the whole family gathered together, it is such a place. If it is a home that serves as a jumping-off point for the whole family to go to church, not just on Sunday morning and not just occasionally, but regularly, it is such a place. If it is a home where the name of God is spoken with reverence and awe and not with disrespect and indifference, it is such a place.

In other words, a house becomes a true home when God is part of the family.

That was my first experience where I saw how Michigan Stadium affected someone else.
-- Fred Jackson on his quarterback's reaction to The Big House

A home is full when all the family members
-- including God -- are present.

OF GOOD CHEER

Read Matthew 21:1-11.

"The crowds that went ahead of him and those that followed shouted" (v. 9).

After enduring a miserable first half of football, the Michigan Stadium crowd did something unexpected when the Wolverines showed up to start the second half: They stood up and cheered.

On Sept. 27, 1997, the national championship wasn't really on anybody's mind when Notre Dame came to Ann Arbor. Sure, UM was 2-0 with convincing wins over Colorado and Baylor, but the Wolverines had started 2-0 the previous three seasons and had wound up losing four games every time.

So the 1-2 Irish stumbled into Ann Arbor and looked tremendous the first half, leading 14-7 at the break.

As writer George Cantor observed, "In other seasons, the big crowd would have been sulking uneasily or sitting in silence." Not this time, though. When the Wolverines showed up after halftime, "the huge throng came to its feet and began to cheer wildly."

Cocaptain and junior tackle Jon Jansen was surprised by the reception. "To feel that kind of energy in the stadium," he said. "I'd never felt it like that before."

As quarterback Brian Griese gathered his charges about him in the huddle, they not only heard the noise but they could feel it. "Every one of us knew then that he could get it done," Jansen said.

Everyone did. Almost immediately Griese hit junior wide receiver Tai Streets on a simple slant pattern across the middle. He sprinted 41 yards for a touchdown to tie the game. The crowd wasn't cheering now; it was screaming.

The defense forced a punt; seven plays later, fullback Chris Floyd scored from the 14. The final score of 21-14 was on the board.

Everything changed that day the crowd stood up and cheered. As Jansen put it, "That's when I knew this year was going to be different." It was quite different; it was a national title season.

Chances are you go to work every day, do your job well, and then go home to your family. This country couldn't run without you; you're indispensable to the nation's efficiency. Even so, nobody cheers for you or waves pompoms in your face. Your name probably will never elicit a standing ovation when a PA announcer calls it.

It's just as well, since public opinion is notoriously fickle. Consider what happened to Jesus. When he entered Jerusalem, he was the object of raucous cheering and an impromptu parade. The crowd's adulation reached such a frenzied pitch that they tore branches off trees and threw their clothes on the ground.

Five days later the crowd shouted again, only this time they screamed for Jesus' execution.

So don't worry too much about not having your personal set of cheering fans. Remember that you do have one personal cheerleader who will never stop pulling for you: God.

We were down and they were cheering like crazy.
— Jon Jansen on the start of the second half vs. Notre Dame

**Just like the sports stars, you do have
a personal cheerleader: God.**

DAY 42

CHEAP TRICKS

Read Acts 19:11-20.

"The evil spirit answered them, 'Jesus I know, and I know about Paul, but who are you?'" (v. 15)

Nuclear physics and a doctor's lab coat. They were just tools for Cecil Pryor's tricks.

Pryor was a starting defensive end in 1968-69 who played for both Bump Elliott and Bo Schembechler. He had fifteen tackles against Southern Cal in the '70 Rose Bowl. On the field, Pryor was described as "big, fast, and aggressive. He played the game with passion." Off the field, he was not averse to a little tomfoolery; he once pulled a trick on the whole nation.

Prior to the '70 Rose Bowl, a television crew came to Ann Arbor to tape the player introductions. Dressed in suit coats and ties, the starters each stepped in front of the camera and gave their name, their hometown, their class, their position, and their major.

Pryor quickly was bored by the whole proceeding and began deliberating on ways to liven this thing up. "I didn't know what I was going to do until the camera came on," he recalled. "As soon as the camera clicked on, it hit me."

So, "as honestly and sincerely as I could," Pryor said, "Hello, my name is Cecil Pryor. I'm from Corpus Christi, Texas, senior, starting right defensive end, and I major in nuclear physics." The guys around him collapsed in laughter because they knew Pryor "hadn't been anywhere near the physics building in his four years at Michigan." The tape played, though, and Pryor even got phone calls from NASA and tickets to come interview for a job.

Schembechler missed the '70 Rose Bowl with a heart attack. At the hospital, doctors would not allow anyone to see him except immediate family, which didn't stop Pryor. He found the doctor's lounge and donned a set of white scrubs and a white lab coat. He then grabbed a clipboard and put a stethoscope around his neck. He went to the room and announced he was Dr. Pryor to see Bo Schembechler. "They just ushered me right on in," Pryor said.

Scam artists love trick plays, but theirs aren't the harmless, funny ones Cecil Pryor pulled off. An e-mail encourages you to send money to some foreign country to get rich. That guy at your front door offers to resurface your driveway at a ridiculously low price. A TV ad promises a pill that lets you lose weight without diet or exercise.

You check things out before deciding. The same approach is necessary with spiritual matters, too, because false religions and bogus Christian denominations abound. The key is always what a group does with Jesus. Is he the Son of God, the ruler of the universe, and the only way to salvation? If not, then what the "church" espouses is something other than the true Word of God.

The good news about Jesus does indeed sound too good to be true. But the only catch is that there is no catch. No trick -- just the truth.

I hung out with him, we chatted for about a half hour, and then I left.
-- Cecil Pryor on his covert visit with Bo Schembechler

God's promises through Jesus sound too good to be true, but the only catch is that there is no catch.

DAY 43

GOOD ADVICE

Read Isaiah 8:11-9:7.

"And he will be called Wonderful Counselor" (v. 9:6b).

John Beilein didn't pay much attention to the advice he got from his uncle -- at first. He eventually built a career on it.

Sometime during the 1986-87 basketball season, a young Beilein met with his athletic director to talk about his team. The college was LeMoyne, a Jesuit school in Syracuse, which was pretty far down the coaching ladder. The athletic director was his uncle.

Beilein didn't like his team's offense very much, so his uncle, a former coach, offered some advice. He suggested that his nephew play offense much like they did in the 1940s. Don't clog the lane with big men but move out to the perimeter. That would open up the floor, making all kinds of cuts and backdoor action possible.

Beilein was polite but he barely listened.

Sometime later, he was casually watching a late-night broadcast of a University of Washington game when he realized that the Huskies were running the offense his uncle had described. Beilein wrote to the head coach and received a stack of mimeographed sheets. He implemented some parts of the offense right away before he switched completely to it in 1987-88. His team went 24-6 and qualified for the Division II NCAA Tournament.

The Beilein offense was born. Over the years, Beilein tinkered with it, constantly writing haphazard notes on anything he could find, including dinner napkins.

WOLVERINES

In 2007, Beilein was named the head coach of the Wolverine men's basketball team. He brought the offense with him. His 2012 team won Michigan's first Big-Ten title in 26 seasons, and Beilein ended the season with 642 wins in his coaching career.

And it really all started with a little advice.

Like John Beilein, we all need a little advice now and then. More often that not, we turn to professional counselors, who are all over the place. Marriage counselors, grief counselors, guidance counselors in our schools, rehabilitation counselors, all sorts of mental health and addiction counselors. No matter what our situation or problem, we can find plenty of advice for the taking.

The problem, of course, is that we find advice easy to offer but hard to swallow. We also have a rueful tendency to solicit the wrong source for advice, seeking counsel that doesn't really solve our problem but that instead enables us to continue with it.

Our need for outside advice, for an independent perspective on our situation, is actually God-given. God serves many functions in our lives, but one role clearly delineated in his Word is that of Counselor. Jesus himself is described as the "Wonderful Counselor." All the advice we need in our lives is right there for the asking; we don't even have to pay for it except with our faith. God is always there for us: to listen, to lead, and to guide.

I don't think you want to listen to what the fans say. If you listen to them too much, you'll be sitting up there with them.
-- Va. Tech football coach Frank Beamer on taking advice from fans

We all need and seek advice in our lives,
but the ultimate and most wonderful Counselor
is of divine and not human origin.

DAY 44

FAIL-SAFE

Read Luke 22:54-62.

"Peter remembered the word the Lord had spoken to him: 'Before the rooster crows today, you will disown me three times.' And he went outside and wept bitterly" (vv. 61b-62).

Rueben Riley was such a failure as a pass receiver that head coach Lloyd Carr called him out for it at his weekly press conference. Good thing Riley was an offensive tackle.

Riley was a regular on the Wolverine offensive line from 2004-06, a three-year letterman who started 27 games. He was honorable mention All-Big Ten as a senior in '06 and went on to play three seasons in the NFL.

On Sept. 23, 2006, Michigan handed Wisconsin its only loss of the season, 27-13. Late in the second quarter, quarterback Chad Henne rifled a pass that a Badger defender deflected right into the arms of a surprised Riley. He cradled the ball and immediately dropped to the ground. The lone reception of his college career resulted in a 9-yard loss.

"I'm very disappointed in Rueben Riley," Carr declared at his next press conference. The remark was a surprise because the head coach was well known for his reluctance to single out players for their mistakes. But Carr went on with his joke, saying, "Rueben and [left tackle] Jake Long have been bugging me since they got here to get a pass to them. . . . So I designed that play to get Rueben a pass, and I don't like what he did with the ball. . . . So that play's out of our playbook."

At least Riley was able to catch the ball. As a junior, he struggled while playing six games with rubber casts on both hands after he fractured his thumbs. That limited his effectiveness against the pass rush. He saw a bright side to it, though; at least he didn't get any holding calls.

Or any pass receptions either.

Failure is usually defined by expectations. Rueben Riley, for instance, was not expected to be a great receiver. A baseball player who hits .300 is a star, but he fails seventy percent of the time. We grumble about a postal system that manages to deliver billions of items without a hitch.

And we are often our own harshest critics, beating ourselves up for our failings because we expected better. Never mind that our expectations were unrealistic to begin with.

The bad news about life is that failure – unlike success -- is inevitable. Only one man walked this earth perfectly and we are certainly not him. The good news about life, however, is that failure isn't permanent. In life, we always have time to reverse our failures as did Peter, he who failed our Lord so abjectly.

The same cannot be said of death. In death we eternally suffer the consequences of our failure to follow that one perfect man.

I saw Rueben catch it and just fall. It was kind of funny at first, but I probably would have done the same thing.
-- Left tackle Jake Long on Rueben Riley's pass reception

**Only one failure in life dooms us to eternal failure
in death: failing to follow Jesus Christ.**

DAY 45

PROBLEM CHILD

Read James 1:2-12.

"Blessed is the man who perseveres under trial, because when he has stood the test, he will receive the crown of life that God has promised to those who love him" (v. 12).

Michigan equipment manager Jon Falk had a big problem: He couldn't find a backup jersey that would let his center go back into the game. He never found it, but he still solved his problem.

George Lilja started every game at center for the Wolverines his junior and senior seasons (1979-80). In 1980, he was a team co-captain along with Anthony Carter. He made one first-team All-America squad and numerous second teams.

After a 1-2 start in 1980, the Wolverines ripped off six straight wins to set up a key showdown with a Purdue squad that would lose only three games that season. One writer said, Lilja "waged the war from center."

He did it with such ferocity that at one point during the game (which Michigan won 26-0 on the way to a win in the Rose Bowl), Lilja's jersey was so ripped up he had to come out and replace it. That sent Falk scurrying, frantically looking for the backup jersey. He pulled out one jersey after another, checking out the numbers while a key member of the offensive line stood helplessly by as the game rolled on without him.

Eventually, a desperate Falk noticed freshman center Doug James standing nearby oblivious to all the activity around him because he was watching the game. Falk walked over to James, pulled his jersey over his head, and handed it to Lilja.

Problem solved.

After the game, an excited friend of James' called him up to say he couldn't believe they had put him in at center in a game as big as Purdue. "I couldn't believe it either," James told him.

Problems are such a ubiquitous feature of our lives that a whole day – twenty-four hours – without a single problem ranks right up there with a government without taxes, a Wolverine team that never, ever loses a game, and entertaining, wholesome television programs. We just can't even imagine it.

But that's life. Even Jesus had his share of problems, especially with his twelve-man staff. Jesus could have easily removed all problems from his daily walk, but what good would that have done us? Our goal is to become like Jesus, and we could never fashion ourselves after a man who didn't encounter job stress, criticism, loneliness, temptation, frustration, and discouragement.

Instead, Jesus showed us that when – not if – problems come, a person of faith uses them to get better rather than letting the problems use him to get bitter. We learn God-filled perseverance and patience as we develop and deepen our faith and our trust in God. Problems will pass; eternity will not.

I am now standing on the bench in front of 105,000 fans at Michigan Stadium with no jersey on in just my shoulder pads and T-shirt.
-- Doug James after Jon Falk solved his problem

**The problem with problems is that we often
let them use us and become bitter
rather than using them to become better.**

DAY 46

ALL IN

Read Mark 12:28-34.

"Love the Lord your God with all your heart and with all your soul and with all your mind and with all your strength" (v. 30).

Band announcer Carl Grapentine's enthusiasm once got the best of him and led him to an embarrassing mistake.

In the fall of 1896, Harry dePont, a 17-year-old student from Ann Arbor, invited all musicians on campus to attend a meeting to organize a band for the University. Nearly thirty musicians gathered on November 13, 1896. The Michigan Marching Band was born out of that meeting.

Over the decades, the band has evolved into one of the nation's premier marching groups and has the hardware to prove it. On January 1, 1983, the band was the first recipient of the Sudler Trophy, awarded to a college marching band for general excellence.

Grapentine served as the band announcer at football games beginning in 1970. Following an 8-1-2 season, the Wolverines were tapped for the 1976 Orange Bowl. The band naturally made the trip to Miami; so did Grapentine.

The unusual press box presented some difficulties for the UM announcer. The announcing booth was enclosed, and Grapentine had to wear a heavy headset. The two factors combined to virtually eliminate the crowd noise from the booth.

Television dictated that the game couldn't begin until the Rose

Bowl ended, and that game ran late. Finally, though, UCLA scored to put the game away and end Ohio State's national title hopes. A man rushed into the booth and declared, "We've got to announce the Rose Bowl score. The fans here don't know." Hooked up for the band's pre-game show, Grapentine said, 'I'll do it."

He did and waited for the roar of the crowd. He got nothing.

Later, Grapentine learned to his dismay that in his enthusiasm, he had given the score right in the middle of the invocation prayer being delivered by the Oklahoma quarterback.

What fills your life, your heart, and your soul so much that you sometimes just can't help what you do? We all have zeal and enthusiasm for something, whether it's Wolverine football, sports cars, our family, scuba diving, or stamp collecting.

But do we have a zeal for the Lord? We may well jump up and down, scream, holler, even cry – generally making a spectacle of ourselves – when Michigan scores. Yet on Sunday morning, if we go to church at all, we probably sit there showing about as much enthusiasm as we would for a root canal.

Of all the divine rules, regulations, and commandments we find in the Bible, Jesus made it crystal clear which one is number one: We are to love God with everything we have. All our heart, all our soul, all our mind, all our strength.

If we do that, our zeal and enthusiasm will burst forth. Like Carl Grapentine, we just won't be able to help ourselves.

Sports Illustrated *called me an overzealous PA announcer.*
-- Carl Grapentine on his Orange Bowl gaffe

**The enthusiasm with which we worship God
reveals the depth of our relationship with him.**

DAY 47

PLAN AHEAD

Read Psalm 33:1-15.

"The plans of the Lord stand firm forever, the purposes of his heart through all generations" (v. 11).

Head coach Matt Anderson had a plan to pull out a win in the last seconds. It just didn't work out.

The Michigan water polo team of 2008 set a program record for wins with its 34-11 record (broken by the 2009 team with a 35-9 slate). During that sterling season, the team also set a program record by winning 27 straight games. No game during the long run was any more exciting than the 6-5 win over 16th-ranked Hartwick College that extended the streak to sixteen games.

The Wolverines were ranked 12th when they hosted Hartwick, and the team spent the night in territory unfamiliar to them during the win streak. They were behind, trailing at halftime for the first time in more than a month.

They rallied, though, and tied the game 5-5 in the last period. That seemed to be all they could muster, however, as the clock steadily ticked away. Finally, with only thirty seconds left to play, Anderson called a time out. He had obviously been doing some serious strategizing since he had a plan for his team. He carefully drew up a play they had never run before and sent them back into the water by saying, "If they give it to us, take it."

Hartwick did give it to them, but not what Anderson expected. With the ball, junior Carrie Frost went looking for senior Michelle

Keeley as her head coach had instructed. All the while, that clock was steadily dropping off the few seconds that were left.

But Hartwick had Keeley covered, so Frost ditched the plan. "I knew I had to drive the ball and take the shot," she said. She did and she did. She moved toward the goal and then let fly. With 15 seconds to play, her shot hit the back of the net for the game-winning goal that drove a roaring Wolverine crowd to its feet.

"It was the greatest game I've ever been a part of," Anderson said. So what if his plan didn't work.

Successful living takes planning. You go to school to improve your chances for a better paying job. You use blueprints to build your home. You plan for retirement. You map out your vacation to have the best time. You even plan your children -- sometimes.

Your best-laid plans, however, sometime get wrecked by events and circumstances beyond your control. The economy goes into the tank; a debilitating illness strikes; a hurricane hits. Life is capricious and sometimes downright ornery. As a result, no plans -- not even your best ones -- are foolproof.

But you don't have to go it alone. God has plans for your life that guarantee success as God defines it if you will make him your planning partner. God's plan for your life includes joy, love, peace, kindness, gentleness, and faithfulness, all the elements necessary for truly successful living for today and for all eternity. And God's plan will not fail.

I realized it wasn't going to work.
-- Carrie Frost on coach Matt Anderson's last-minute plan

Your plans may ensure a successful life;
God's plans will ensure a successful eternity.

WINNER'S CIRCLE

Read 1 John 5:1-12.

"Who is it that overcomes the world? Only he who believes that Jesus is the Son of God" (v. 5).

Roger Zatkoff wanted Michigan to win so badly that he took himself out of the biggest game of his life.

Recruiting in the fall of 1947 was not exactly what it is today. The rules prevented schools from providing transportation, so when the Michigan coaches wanted Zatkoff to make a visit, he had to make his own way. He hitchhiked to and from the game.

He made it to the stadium, found his way to the tunnel, and stood around until someone told him to go find himself a seat. He wandered into The Big House and wound up sitting in the south end zone. Michigan whipped Pittsburgh 69-0 that day. As Zatkoff put it, "I hosted myself on my recruiting trip."

He was a good enough host that he committed to Michigan. As a sophomore in 1950, he started the first game at linebacker and held the spot all three seasons. Zatkoff was a participant in the infamous "Snow Bowl" of 1950. (See Devotion No. 70.) He had injured a knee the week before, so he stood on the sideline and handed out hand warmers to his teammates coming off the field.

The 9-3 win over Ohio State clinched a berth in the 1951 Rose Bowl. Zatkoff's knee was better after the long layoff, but he reinjured it in the first half. He finished the half but realized his mobility was too limited for him to be effective. Zatkoff put winning ahead of personal glory and hunted up his position coach at halftime. He told him he could play but the team would be better with his substitute, Ted Topor, in the game. Zatkoff stayed on the sideline as Michigan came from behind to beat Cal 14-6.

As a senior in 1952, Zatkoff was All-Big Ten. In 1985, he was inducted into the UM Athletic Hall of Fame. In 1991, the school established the Roger Zatkoff Award, given each year to the team's most outstanding linebacker.

Life itself, not just athletic events, is a competition. You vie against other job applicants. You seek admission to a college with a limited number of open spots. You compete against others for a date. Sibling rivalry is real; just ask your brother or sister.

Inherent in any competition or in any situation that involves wining and losing is an antagonist. You always have an opponent to overcome, even if it's an inanimate video game, a golf course, or even yourself.

Nobody wants to be numbered among life's losers. We recognize them when we see them, and maybe mutter a prayer that says something like, "There but for the grace of God go I."

But one adversary will defeat us: Death will claim us all. We can turn the tables on this foe, though; we can defeat the grave. A victory is possible, however, only through faith in Jesus Christ. With Jesus, we have hope beyond death because we have life.

With Jesus, we win. For all of eternity.

The game was too crucial.
        -- Roger Zatkoff on why he told the coaches to put his backup in

**Death is the ultimate opponent;
Jesus is the ultimate victor.**

DAY 49

THE INTERVIEW

Read Romans 14: 1-12.

"We will all stand before God's judgment seat. . . . So then, each of us will give an account of himself to God"
(vv. 10, 12).

One shabby, insulting, 40-minute interview changed the history of Michigan football.

After the 1966 football season, Wisconsin sought out the head coach at Miami of Ohio, who had won two straight league titles, about becoming their head coach. He was Bo Schembechler, who, not surprisingly, was interested in what would be a move into the Big Ten and really big-time college football. He went to Madison for an interview at the unusual hour of 10 p.m. on a Sunday.

Schembechler arrived "to face 20 guys sitting around a room, looking bored." One of the committee members fell asleep during the interview. Another was a student who, Schembechler recalled, asked smart-aleck questions. The fiasco lasted forty minutes. The future coaching legend left the room, found the nearest pay phone, called the Wisconsin athletic director, and told him to withdraw his name from consideration.

The only positive to come out of the fiasco worked to Michigan's advantage. Schembechler resolved to coach in the Big Ten and to reject other feelers until he got the chance. It came in 1968 with a phone call from Bump Elliott, Michigan's outgoing coach who was recruiting his successor.

Schembechler was interested, but he had some stipulations: There would be no dog-and-pony show. "Michigan didn't need some silly committee or student rep to check me out," he said, "and I didn't need any dime-store tour of the campus to appreciate what Michigan had to offer."

Only two days after that phone call, Schembechler and Elliott sealed a deal with a handshake. UM football history was about to be made. That the coach was even available was thanks in part to Wisconsin's lousy interview process.

You know about job interviews. You've experienced the stress, the anxiety, the helpless feeling that's part of any interview. You tried to appear calm and relaxed while struggling to come up with reasonably original answers to banal questions and to hide your considered opinion that the interviewer was a total geek. You told yourself that if they turned you down, it was their loss.

You won't be so indifferent or nonchalant, though, about your last interview: the one with God. A day will come when we will all stand before God to account for ourselves. It is to God and God alone – not our friends, not our parents, not society in general – that we must give a final and complete account.

Since all eternity will be at stake, it sure would help to have a surefire reference with you. One – and only one -- is available: Jesus Christ.

If I was in your shoes, I wouldn't go to Wisconsin.
-- Bo Schembechler's advice to a young Bobby Knight

You will have one last interview
-- with God -- and you sure want Jesus
there with you as a character witness.

DAY 50

CELEBRATION TIME

Read Luke 15:1-10.

"There is rejoicing in the presence of the angels of God over one sinner who repents" (v. 10).

Michigan fans always celebrate after a win over Ohio State. In 2003, though, they did it on the field.

Earlier in the week of the game of Nov. 22, an e-mail circulated on the UM campus that urged students to rush the field after the Wolverines whipped the Buckeyes. It even gave directions for an orderly scaling of the red brick wall that separates the seats and the playing field in Michigan Stadium. "Just start heading down, because that'll force people in front of you to do so and then the momentum can't be stopped," the message instructed.

Not surprisingly, university officials were not too happy and fired off their own e-mail, asking students not to mar the celebration by risking injury on the playing field. "The wall doesn't move," the counter-e-mail declared.

Oh, but the Wolverines did, rolling up 35 points in the historic 100th meeting between the two programs. When star tailback Chris Perry scored his second TD of the game, this one from the 15 with 7:55 to play, the final of 35-21 was on the scoreboard.

With the clock down to zero, the celebration began as joyful Wolverine fans poured onto the field. Interestingly enough, they did so in an orderly fashion, waiting quite patiently for those in front of them to move down to the wall. There, they assisted each other over the wall and onto the field where the celebration began in earnest. Fans mobbed the Wolverine players, especially Perry, who had to struggle to get into the tunnel and the locker room. "Our fans were rougher out there than OSU's defense," he joked.

The fans were in no hurry to leave the field, ignoring the pleas from the public address announcer to head home. The voice had a sense of humor about it all, declaring, "Those of you who think you are on TV; you are not."

They didn't care. They were just celebrating.

Michigan just whipped Ohio State. You got that new job or that promotion. You just held your newborn child in your arms. Life has those grand moments that call for celebration. You may jump up and down and scream in a wild frenzy at a UM game or share a quiet, sedate candlelight dinner at home -- but you celebrate.

Consider then a celebration beyond our imagining, one that fills every corner of the very home of God and the angels. Imagine a celebration in Heaven, which also has its grand moments.

Those grand moments are touched off when someone comes to faith in Jesus. Heaven itself rings with the joyous sounds of the singing and dancing of the celebrating angels. Even God rejoices when just one person – you or someone you have introduced to Christ? -- turns to him.

When you said "yes" to Christ, you made the angels dance.

I was worried I was going to get injured with them celebrating.
        -- Chris Perry on the postgame celebration in 2003

**God himself joins the angels in heavenly
celebration when even a single person
turns to him through faith in Jesus.**

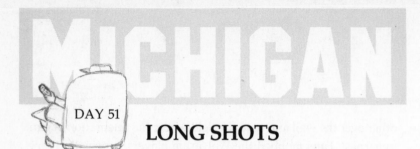

DAY 51

LONG SHOTS

Read Matthew 9:9-13.

"[Jesus] saw a man named Matthew sitting at the tax collector's booth. 'Follow me,' he told him, and Matthew got up and followed him" (v. 9).

They started out favorites, played themselves into being long shots to win anything, and wound up as national champions.

Big things were expected of Michigan's 2001 field hockey team, but it failed to win either the Big Ten regular season title or the tournament. The Wolverines even lost twice to Ohio State. Their 14-5 record earned them an at-large berth in the NCAA Tournament where they were underdogs in the opening round against North Carolina, a team they had never beaten.

Perhaps, though, the Wolverines had UNC whipped before the game even began. UM hosted the regional, and the teams arrived to find a coating of ice on the field. "The North Carolina players were aghast." Sophomore forward April Fronzoni, a two-time All-America, said the look on the Tar Heels' faces would forever be etched in her memory. Michigan won easily 5-2.

When Catherine Foreman scored in overtime to nudge Michigan State 2-1, the long shots were on their way to the NCAA semifinals. Princeton was the opponent, and the players regarded the Wolverines with such disdain that throughout their 40 minutes of warm-up, they asked each other, "Where's Michigan?"

Michigan missed the insult, however. The team was caught in

a traffic jam and arrived only minutes before game time. "So we get there and we stroll across the field in our flip-flops," recalled coach Marcia Pankratz. Michigan won 4-2.

They were really long shots in the finals against Maryland, the top-ranked team in the country. But goalkeeper Maureen Tasch played the game of her life, setting a school record with her eighth shutout of the season. The long shots won 2-0, becoming the first Michigan women's varsity athletic team to win a national title.

Like UM's field hockey team in 2001, Matthew the tax collector was a long shot. In his case, he was an unlikely person to be a confidant of the Son of God. While we may not get all warm and fuzzy about the IRS, our government's revenue agents are nothing like Matthew and his ilk. He bought a franchise, paying the Roman Empire for the privilege of extorting, bullying, and stealing everything he could from his own people. Tax collectors of that time were "despicable, vile, unprincipled scoundrels."

And yet, Jesus said only two words to this lowlife: "Follow me." Jesus knew that this long shot would make an excellent disciple.

It's the same with us. While we may not be quite as vile as Matthew was, none of us can stand before God with our hands clean and our hearts pure. We are all impossibly long shots to enter God's Heaven. That is, until we do what Matthew did: get up and follow Jesus.

What it came down to was that we had the best team.
-- Two-time All-American Kristi Gannon on the Maryland win

**Only through Jesus does our status change
from being long shots to enter God's Kingdom
to being heavy favorites.**

DAY 52

ONE-MAN ARMY

Read Revelation 19:11-21.

"The rest of them were killed by the sword that came out of the mouth of the rider on the horse" (v. 21).

Against Ohio State in 1940 Tom Harmon was such a one-man army that the Buckeye fans gave him a standing ovation.

Harmon has been called "quite possibly the best college football player ever." He had matinee-idol looks that landed him on the covers of both *Life* and *Time* magazines. The latter publication called him a "gregarious, lantern-jawed six-footer with a Tarzan physique" After he graduated, Harmon starred in a Hollywood movie -- about himself.

Incredibly, Harmon lived up to all the hype. Against Cal, he took the opening kickoff of the 1940 season 94 yards for a touchdown. On his first carry from scrimmage, he went 86 yards for six points. He then went 70 and 65 yards for touchdowns. Obviously disturbed that no one could stop the Heisman-Trophy winning halfback, an inebriated Cal fan made his way onto the field and tried to tackle him. Naturally, he failed.

But the most extraordinary performance of Harmon's career came in his last game, against Ohio State in Columbus. Playing in the rain on a muddy field, he scored two rushing touchdowns, threw two passing touchdowns, kicked four extra points, intercepted three passes and ran one back for a touchdown, returned three kickoffs for 81 yards, and punted three times for an average of 50 yards. His 34 points was a collegiate record.

The Wolverines trounced Ohio State 40-0, but Harmon's game had been so spectacular that when he left the field with 38 seconds left, the Buckeye fans stood *en masse* to applaud him. Several even rushed onto the field just to touch him or to attempt to get a piece of his jersey. They didn't get much because it was so torn up he had no sleeves left.

Even Buckeyes appreciated the one-man army from Michigan.

A similar situation will occur when Christ returns. He will not come back to us as the meek lamb led unprotestingly to slaughter on the cross. Instead, he will be a one-man army, a rider on a white horse who will destroy those forces responsible for disorder and chaos in God's world.

This image of our Jesus as a warrior may well shock and discomfort us; it should also excite and thrill us. It reminds us vividly that God will unleash his awesome power to effect justice and righteousness in a world that persecutes his people and slanders his name. It should also lend us a sense of urgency because the time will pass when decisions for Christ can still be made.

For now, Jesus has an army at his disposal in the billions of Christians around the world. We are Christian soldiers; we have a world to conquer for our Lord – before he returns as a one-man army to finish the job.

When you get that from their fans, and you're a Michigan man, it's pretty special. That was a great thrill for all of us.
  -- Forest Evashevski on Tom Harmon's standing ovation in Columbus

Jesus will return as a one-man army to conquer the forces of evil; for now, we are his army.

DAY 53

HOW DISAPPOINTING

Read Ezra 3.

*"Many of the older priests and Levites and family heads,
who had seen the former temple, wept aloud when they
saw the foundation of this temple being laid, while many
others shouted for joy" (v. 12).*

Tom Mack's sophomore season at Michigan ended with such bitter disappointment that he called it "the most embarrassing incident in my life as a football player."

Mack figured he drew interest from Michigan primarily because he was from Cleveland and UM needed someone from the area on the team to help recruit others. His high-school coaches also convinced a recruiter he would get bigger and better.

After all, as Mack admitted, "I was not a particularly good high school football player." That may have been an exaggeration. Mack had terrible vision but didn't play with glasses. He played both ways at end and couldn't catch the ball on offense because he couldn't see it. He had to listen for it, which didn't work too well "because the only time I heard it was when it went by me, or when it hit the ground."

At Michigan, the team bought him some contact lenses, and in 1963, his sophomore year, he worked his way up to second team. Against Ohio State, head coach Bump Elliott called out, "Second team, get ready to go in." He went down the line of the players, putting a hand on their shoulders, giving them a shove toward the field, and saying, "In, in, in." When he came to Mack, though, he said, "Sit down!" "I was absolutely crushed," Mack said.

That was about the last such disappointment of Mack's football career. In the spring, the coaches moved him to offensive tackle. As a senior in 1965, he was All-America and then was the No. 1 pick of the Los Angeles Rams. He went on to an All-Pro career and was inducted into the Pro Football Hall of Fame in 1999.

We know disappointment. Friends lie to us or betray us; we lose our jobs through no fault of our own; emotional distance grows between us and our children; the Wolverines get beat; our dreams shatter.

Disappointment occurs when something or somebody fails to meet our expectations, which inevitably will happen. What is crucial to our life, therefore, is not avoiding disappointment but handling it.

One alternative is to act as the old people of Israel did at the dedication of the temple. Instead of joyously celebrating the construction of a new place of worship, they wailed and moaned about the lost glories of the old one. They chose disappointment over lost glories rather than the wonders of the present reality.

Disappointment can paralyze us all, but only if we lose sight of an immutable truth: Our lives may not always be what we wish they were, but God is still good to us.

There's nothing disappointing about that.

That was the highlight, or lowlight, of my sophomore year.
-- Tom Mack on not getting to play against Ohio State

Even in disappointing times, we can be confident that God is with us and therefore life is good.

DAY 54

BAD IDEA

Read Mark 14:43-50.

"The betrayer had arranged a signal with them: 'The one I kiss is the man; arrest him and lead him away under guard'" (v. 44).

Drew Dileo had a very good idea when he decided to play football for Michigan. Sitting in a Louisiana lake, though, he once had a very bad idea involving an alligator.

In August 2011, the sophomore wide receiver was on a fishing trip back home with a buddy when they hooked an alligator. Dileo suggested they reel it in. His friend replied, "You get it in the boat. I'm going to grab it by its mouth and put a tape around it."

So Dileo set about reeling the gator in until it opened its mouth to reveal a whole bunch of extremely threatening teeth. "We're changing the plan," Dileo said, which was a much better idea.

Coming out of high school, Dileo was not a hot football prospect. But veteran UM coach Fred Jackson, who was born in Louisiana five miles from Dileo's mother, recruited the state. On a visit to Dileo's high school, he watched some film and saw an athlete short on physical makeup but long on talent and desire.

Jackson decided he wanted Dileo, who, strangely enough considering where he was from, was a lifelong Michigan fan. When he was 8 years old, he had asked Santa for a Michigan comforter.

Dileo didn't play much in 2010, making only one catch, but as a sophomore in 2011, he became a sure-handed option in offensive coordinator Al Borges' wide-open system.

After the 2011 season, Dileo got a little special treatment from his fellow Louisianan come bowl time. He was in an airport in North Carolina headed home when Jackson called him with some big news. "I'm going to tell you something no one else knows," he said. "We're headed home. We're going to play in the Sugar Bowl."

Which for Drew Dileo was a really good idea.

That sure-fire investment you made from a pal's hot stock tip. The expensive exercise machine that now traps dust bunnies under your bed. Blonde hair. Telling your wife you wanted to eat at the restaurant with the waitresses in the skimpy shorts. They seemed like pretty good ideas at the time; they weren't.

We all have bad ideas in our lifetime. They provide some of our most crucial learning experiences. For instance, Drew Dileo has probably never again seriously considered putting his hands down an unhappy alligator's mouth.

Some ideas, though, are so irreparably and inherently bad that we cannot help but wonder why they were even conceived in the first place. Almost two thousand years ago a man had just such an idea. Judas' betrayal of Jesus for a few pieces of silver remains to this day among the most heinous acts of treachery in history.

Turning his back on Jesus was a bad idea for Judas then; it's a bad idea for us now.

There's no way I'm putting my hands down there.
— Drew Dileo on the very bad idea of getting a gator into the boat

We all have some pretty bad ideas
during our lifetime, but nothing equals
the folly of turning away from Jesus.

THE CHALLENGE

Read Matthew 4:12-25.

"Come, follow me," Jesus said (v. 19).

Every time Karlee Bruck took the court for the Michigan volleyball team, she faced a challenge no one else did.

After Bruck arrived in Ann Arbor for preseason camp in 2007, she noticed how thirsty she was. "I was drinking so much water and Gatorade that it was unreal," she recalled. She put it down to the challenge and excitement of her first days as a college athlete. She got tired frequently and attributed it to jet lag and tough practices. Her vision fluctuated; she figured she needed glasses.

When a concerned head coach Mark Rosen asked her if she had an eating disorder, Bruck just laughed. "I thought that was pretty funny," she said, "because me and food, I love it." But Rosen was dead serious. He pointed out that she was losing weight, and he talked her into going to the doctor.

The news that came back was a shocker; Bruck had diabetes. After a brief interval of panic, she knew what she had to do: Get healthy and play volleyball again. There was no other option.

She was redshirted that season and spent the time getting a handle on her condition. She found that she preferred the convenience and the reliability of an insulin pump, which presented a challenge to someone who spends a lot of time earnestly diving and jumping around on a volleyball court.

Other diabetic athletes took their pumps off during games and practices, but Bruck's blood sugar shot sky-high when she tried that. "I found something that works," she said. She hooked her pump to the back of her spandex shorts. "I didn't care if it was going to hurt or not," she said. "I wanted to play volleyball."

And Bruck did. Wearing that pump clipped to the back of her shorts all the while, she lettered for four seasons (2008-11). In 2008, she set a school single-match record for attack percentage.

As Karlee Bruck is, we all are challenged daily. Life is a testing ground; God intentionally set it up that way. If we are to grow in character, confidence, and perseverance, and if we are to make a difference in the world, we must meet challenges head-on. Few things in life are as boring and as destructive to our sense of self-worth as a job that doesn't offer any challenges.

Our faith life is the same way. The moment we answered Jesus' call to "Come, follow me," we took on the most difficult challenge we will ever face. We are called to be holy by walking in Jesus' footsteps in a world that seeks to render our Lord irrelevant and his influence negligible. The challenge Jesus places before us is to put our faith and our trust in him and not in ourselves or the transitory values of the secular world.

Daily walking in Jesus' footsteps is a challenge, but the path takes us all the way right up to the gates of Heaven – and then right on through.

I started to panic at first, but at the same time, I knew this was going to be something that I had to take the reins of and get control of.
-- Karlee Bruck on learning she had diabetes

To accept Jesus as Lord is to joyfully take on the challenge of living a holy life in an unholy world.

DAY 56

LESSON LEARNED

Read Psalm 143.

"Teach me to do your will, for you are my God" (v. 10).

Brian Townsend used a lesson he learned as a Michigan football player to help him through a heartrending tragedy.

Townsend was a linebacker in Ann Arbor from 1988-91, playing on four Big Ten champions and in three Rose Bowls. In 2007, he was hired as UM's Director of Basketball Operations.

After he played two seasons in the NFL, Townsend returned to Michigan to earn a second degree. He met Rachael, they fell in love, and they married in 1998. In October 2003, they were in Chicago for Rachael to run the Chicago Marathon. She was 29, an elite athlete, a soccer coach, and a college dance instructor. She finished 27 seconds ahead of the time she needed to qualify for the Boston Marathon, which was her goal.

Townsend and some friends gathered near the finish line to celebrate the milestone with her. She didn't show up. Almost an hour passed before Brian's cell phone rang. The caller was a doctor from a nearby hospital. It was about Rachael. After she crossed the finish line, she had collapsed from a heart murmur no one had been aware of; she was dead by the time she hit the ground.

Townsend plunged into depression and grief but eventually used a lesson the Michigan coaches taught him to help him make it through the aftermath of the tragedy. It was "sudden change."

Townsend said "sudden change" occurs when the defense gets

a stop deep in its own territory and comes off the field relaxed and triumphant, only to have the offense immediately turn the ball over. The UM coaches always taught the defense not to whine about the trouble they were in but to accept the challenge, to get out of the awful situation with a field goal or no score at all.

For Brian Townsend, the sudden change in his life was like the sudden change on the football field. With the attitude he used to meet the change on the field, he met the challenge of Rachael's death and put his life back together.

Learning about anything requires a combination of education and experience. Education is the accumulation of facts that we call knowledge; experience is the acquisition of wisdom and discernment, which add purpose and understanding to knowledge.

The most difficult way to learn is trial and error: dive in blindly and mess up. The best way to learn is through example coupled with a set of instructions: Someone has gone ahead to show you the way and has written down the information you need to follow.

In teaching us the way we are to live godly lives, God chose the latter method. He set down in his book the habits, actions, and attitudes that make for a way of life in accordance with his tenets and his wishes. He also sent us Jesus to explain and to illustrate.

God teaches us not only how to exist but how to live. We just need to be attentive students.

This is a matter of sudden change. I've got to adapt and look at this as a challenge.
— Brian Townsend on coping with the tragedy of his wife's death

To learn from Jesus is to learn what life is all about and how God means for us to live it.

CAN'T STAND IT!

Read Exodus 32:1-20.

*"[Moses'] anger burned and he threw the tablets out
of his hands, breaking them to pieces at the foot of the
mountain" (v. 19).*

Steve Watson set a rather interesting record during his time as a Wolverine football player. All it got him, though, were seasons full of frustration.

Watson was ranked among the top twenty tight ends in the country when he signed to play for Michigan. "I thought I was on my way," he said, but it just didn't turn out like that.

He injured his knee his freshman year and redshirted in 2007. That was frustration enough, but then his head coach, Lloyd Carr, retired and was replaced by Rich Rodriguez, who had no use for a tight end in his offense.

Thus in the fall of 2008, the offensive coordinator called Watson into his office and told him he had no chance at all of ever playing at Michigan. The coach suggested the tight end transfer.

Watson called it the worst day of his football career.

He did not transfer, but he didn't play much in 2008 either, getting in four games on the special teams unit.

Watson got a break prior to the 2009 season when Greg Robinson was hired as the new defensive coordinator. He had known Watson since childhood. The new coach suggested Watson move to linebacker. He did, figuring he'd get some playing time, but all

WOLVERINES

he got was more frustration.

Watson later moved to defensive end, then defensive tackle. He was a senior in 2011 when head coach Brady Hoke asked him to play fullback after John McColgan was injured. During his career, Watson saw action at five different positions, a school record.

That wasn't the kind of record Watson had expected to set because that game of football musical chairs earned him only four starts in only 29 games. "It's frustrating," he admitted.

The traffic light catches you when you're running late for work or your doctor's appointment. The bureaucrat gives you red tape when you want assistance. Your daughter refuses to take her homework seriously. Makes your blood boil, doesn't it?

Frustration is part of God's testing ground that is life, even if much of what frustrates us today results from man-made organizations, bureaucracies, and machines. What's important is not that you encounter frustration but how you handle it. Do you respond with curses, screams, and violence? Or with a deep breath, a silent prayer, and calm persistence, and patience?

It may be difficult to imagine Jesus stuck in traffic or waiting for hours in a long line in a government office. It is not difficult, however, to imagine how he would act in such situations, and, thus, to know exactly how you should respond. No matter how frustrated you are.

When you start to feel like you're getting good at something, and then you have to learn everything all over again, that's hard.
-- Steve Watson on the frustration of position changes

Frustration is a vexing part of life,
but God expects us to handle it gracefully.

DAY 58

SHAPE UP

Read Luke 12:35-40.

"You also must be ready, because the Son of Man will come at an hour when you do not expect him" (v. 40).

Michigan head coach Fielding Yost was sincerely concerned about his team's stamina for the first-ever Rose Bowl. Apparently his worries were needless. The Wolverines blasted Stanford 49-0 without using a single substitute.

The Wolverines of 1901 were known as the "Point-A Minute" team. They went 11-0 and outscored their opponents 550-0. The team actually averaged better than a point a minute since several games were cut short because an opponent conceded.

When the season ended, Yost agreed to play in the first-ever Rose Bowl game against his former Stanford team. The temperature was ten degrees below zero when the team left Ann Arbor and a balmy eighty-five when the Wolverines arrived in Pasadena.

Concerned about the heat and the month-long layoff, Yost practiced his team hard. He tried to persuade Stanford's coach to shorten the 35-minute halves by ten minutes each, but he refused.

It was Stanford who gave out. The game was scoreless for the first 22 minutes until Michigan scored three times late in the half. Then the Stanford defense wilted in the last half until at one point the Stanford coach asked Yost to cancel the rest of the game. Yost refused. Finally, with eight minutes left and Michigan up 49-0, the Stanford captain said to his counterpart, Hugh White, "If you

WOLVERINES

are willing, we are ready to quit." The Wolverines accepted.

Yost didn't use any of his three subs. After the game, the team was celebrating in the hotel when Yost noticed they were missing. He asked guard Dan McGugin and halfback Willie Heston (UM's third All-America) to look them up. They found the trio out back turning a garden hose on each other and rolling around in the mud in their uniform. They said they didn't want to go home and have it known they hadn't played.

Like a football game against a tough, physical opponent, life is an endurance sport; you're in it for the long haul. So you schedule a physical, check your blood pressure for free at the supermarket pharmacy, walk or jog, and hop on the treadmill that hides under the bed or doubles as a coat rack.

The length of your life, however, is really the short haul when compared to the long haul that is eternity. To prepare yourself for eternity requires conditioning that is spiritual rather than physical. Jesus prescribed a regimen so his followers could be in tip-top spiritual shape. It requires not just occasional exercise but a way of living every day that includes abiding faith, decency, witnessing, mercy, trust, and generosity.

If a UM team isn't ready when the opposition kicks off, it loses a game. If you aren't ready when Jesus calls, you lose eternity.

Proper conditioning is that fleeting moment between getting ready and going stale.
-- Alabama coach Frank Thomas

Physical conditioning is good for the short run,
but you also need to be in peak spiritual shape
for the long haul.

CLOCKWORK

Read Matthew 25:1-13.

"Keep watch, because you do not know the day or the hour" (v. 13).

When Bo Schembechler coached Michigan, his players didn't live under the restraints of the same time zone as the other residents of Ann Arbor. They followed BST, Bo Schembechler Time.

As the coach's players quickly came to understand, his personal clock -- and thus their own -- ran ten minutes ahead of everyone else's. To stay on BST was insurance against having to run extra laps for being late to a team function.

Calvin O'Neal learned the hard way the repercussions of not living on BST. O'Neal is one of the greatest linebackers in Wolverine history. He was All-America in 1976. Against Purdue that season, he had 24 tackles, a UM record that still stands.

On a trip for a Wisconsin game, when O'Neal and a few other players arrived at the banquet room for a team meal, everyone was already eating. They knew they were in the doghouse.

Defensive coordinator Gary Moeller saw the players standing in the hall and fetched them with directions to "come on in and sit down, and be quiet." But O'Neal knew quite well just getting to a table wouldn't be the end of it, so the players came up with a story get them out of trouble. They told Schembechler they had been on the elevator on their way to dinner when "this obese lady fell in the elevator and broke her leg." They had called 911 and then helped the medics get her out of the elevator.

Schembechler listened to their whopper and did nothing -- at the time. But at the team meeting on Sunday in Ann Arbor after the win, he called O'Neal to the front and told him to "tell this team that cock-a-mamey story that you told me." So to his embarrassment, O'Neal had to repeat the tale to the team, while the whole bunch "died laughing. . . . I mean they were on the floor."

O'Neal and his fellow conspirators had to run every day after practice the rest of the season both for losing track of Bo Schembechler Time and for coming up with such an awful excuse.

We may pride ourselves on our time management, but the truth is that we don't manage time; it manages us. Hurried and harried, we live by schedules that seem to have too much what and too little when. By setting the bedside alarm at night, we even let the clock determine how much down time we get. A life of leisure actually means one in which time is of no importance.

Every second of our life -- all the time we have – is a gift from God, who dreamed up time in the first place. We would do well, therefore, to consider what God considers to be good time management. After all, Jesus himself warned us against mismanaging the time we have. From God's point of view, using our time wisely means being prepared at every moment for Jesus' return, which will occur -- well, only time will tell when.

The worst thing you could do with Bo was be late.

– Calvin O'Neal

**We mismanage our time when we fail
to prepare for Jesus' return even though
we don't know when that will be.**

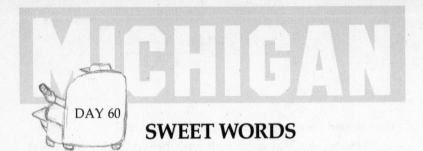

DAY 60

SWEET WORDS

Read Romans 8:28-39.

"In all these things we are more than conquerors through him who loved us" (v. 37).

Mike Matheny prayed for some affirmation for a decision he had just made. He got it in the form of pigeon poop and a field hockey player.

When Michigan offered Matheny a baseball scholarship his senior year of high school, he quickly accepted. His life got complicated, though, when the Toronto Blue Jays drafted him in June. Matheny initially reaffirmed his commitment to Michigan, but Toronto wouldn't go away. Even after he arrived on campus, they repeatedly called his dorm room to up their offer.

Matheny had until the moment he actually attended his first class to accept the Blue Jays' offer. He prayed a lot over his decision and wanted a sign of some sort, but "[I] didn't know what exactly I was looking for in return."

Finally, the morning of his first class arrived. He put his backpack on, and just before he walked out the door, he called the Jays and told them he was playing baseball for Michigan.

Matheny started having second thoughts as soon as he left his dorm room. Then he got a sign from above -- just not the one he was looking for. A load of pigeon poop landed squarely on his head. "The pigeon was apparently the size of a turkey," he said.

He had to return to his room to shower and change, which

gave him more time to think everything over. Strangely enough, the whole laughable incident with the pigeon poop served to re-affirm his decision, to serve as a sign he had chosen correctly.

Then when he made it to class, he received his second affirma-tion. He met what he called a "hot blonde" named Kristin who was on the field hockey team. She became his wife.

Matheny played catcher for Michigan from 1989-92 and was a team captain in '92. He went on to a 13-year major-league career.

Like Mike Matheny, you make a key decision. You tell your best friend or your spouse and await a reaction. "Boy, that was dumb" is the answer you get. Or a friend's life spirals downward. Do you pretend you don't know that messed-up person?

Everybody needs affirmation in some degree. That is, we all occasionally need someone to say something positive about us, that we are worth something, and that God loves us.

The follower of Jesus does what our Lord did when he encoun-tered someone whose life was a mess. Rather than seeing what they were, he saw what they could become. Life is hard; it breaks us all to some degree. To be like Jesus, we see past the problems of the broken and the hurting and envision their potential, under-standing that not condemning is not condoning.

The Christian's words of affirmation are the greatest, most joyous of all. They constitute a message of victory and triumph from which nothing can separate us or defeat us.

God, I've asked you to be clear before, but c'mon.
-- Mike Matheny on the pigeon poop

The greatest way to affirm lost persons
is to lead them to Christ.

DAY 61

FAMILY TIES

Read Mark 3:31-35.

*"[Jesus] said, 'Here are my mother and my brothers!
Whoever does God's will is my brother and sister and
mother'" (vv. 34-35).*

Mark Messner had decided to play his college football in California -- and then he started thinking about his family.

From 1985-88, Messner, a defensive tackle, made All-Big Ten, only the third player in league history to be a four-time all-star. He was also a two-time All-America. He still holds the Michigan records for tackles for loss (70) and yards lost (376).

Messner's collegiate career got off to a rather interesting start. In the '85 season opener against Notre Dame (a 20-12 win), he got down in his stance for his first play and promptly vomited on the hands of the offensive lineman opposite him. "He couldn't move," Messner recalled. "The ball was snapped while he was still looking at the mess on his hands." With the lineman rather preoccupied, Messner made the tackle for a two-yard loss.

Messner wasn't always a sure thing to play his football in Ann Arbor. In fact, for a brief time, he decided on UCLA.

Attending an all-male school in Detroit, Messner had never seen anything like the UCLA campus when he made a recruiting trip in December of 1983. He traded the cold and snow of Detroit for the sun of Southern California. "There were bathing suits and roller skates," he recalled. "When we walked the campus,

WOLVERINES

it looked like a botanical garden." Messner said, "I convinced myself that I was going to put myself first and come to California to have a good time." But he wound up putting his family first.

When Messner landed in Detroit, he told his parents, "I'm a Bruin." During the night, though, he had second thoughts. Maybe he should stay closer to home so his stepdad, who had cancer, could see him play.

The next morning, Messner called Michigan to tell them of his decision. Then he blurted out to his surprised parents, "I'm a Wolverine." Family had won out.

Some wit said families are like fudge, mostly sweet with a few nuts. You can probably call the names of your sweetest relatives, whom you cherish, and of the nutty ones too, whom you mostly try to avoid at a family reunion. Like it or not, you have a family, and that's God's doing. God cherishes the family so much that he chose to live in one as a son, a brother, and a cousin.

One of Jesus' more startling actions was to redefine the family. No longer is it a single household of blood relatives or even a clan or a tribe. Jesus' family is the result not of an accident of birth but rather a conscious choice. All those who do God's will are members of Jesus' family.

What a startling and downright wonderful thought! You have family members out there you don't even know who stand ready to love you just because you're part of God's family.

My dad was able to see my entire career. He died in 1989.
-- Mark Messner on his family and his football

For followers of Jesus, family comes not
from a shared ancestry but from a shared faith.

DAY 62

BIG DEAL

Read Ephesians 3:1-13.

"His intent was that now, through the church, the manifold wisdom of God should be made known" (v. 10).

Becoming the all-time leading rusher in school history is a big deal, but for Anthony Thomas the most important run he made all night came after the game was over.

On Jan. 1, 2001, the Wolverines, cochamps of the Big Ten, completed a 9-3 season with a hard-fought 31-28 win over Auburn in the Citrus Bowl in Orlando. After Michigan scored early, Auburn responded with a pair of touchdowns in the second quarter to lead 14-7.

From then on, the game belonged to Michigan. The Wolverines scored three straight touchdowns, and led 21-14 at halftime and 31-21 after three quarters. Though quarterback Drew Henson threw for 294 yards, Thomas' legs carried UM to the win.

The senior, who passed up the NFL for the chance to complete his degree, entered the game needing 106 yards rushing to pass Jamie Morris (1984-87) as the school's all-time leading rusher. Since Auburn's sturdy defense was built to stop the run, whether Thomas would get the record was questionable. Not for long.

In the second quarter, Thomas gave Michigan the lead for good with an 11-yard touchdown run that broke the school record. He had 182 yards and two touchdowns for the night and was the bowl game's MVP. He finished his Michigan career with 4,472 yards rushing.

But it was after the game ended that Thomas made a really big run. With the game ball tucked under one arm, he made his way through the throng of happy teammates and jogged to a corner of the end zone. There, he delivered the ball to his jubilant wife, Hayley. "I wanted to give her something to let her know how I feel," the new UM record-holder explained on this their 10-month anniversary.

Like Anthony Thomas' rushing record, "big deals" are important components of the unfolding of our lives. Our wedding, the birth of a child, a new job, a new house, big Michigan games, even a new car. In many ways, what we regard as a big deal is what shapes not only our lives but our character.

One of the most unfathomable anomalies of faith in America today is that while many people profess to be die-hard Christians, they disdain involvement with a local church. As Paul tells us, however, the Church is a very big deal to God; it is at the heart of his redemptive work; it is a vital part of his eternal purposes.

The Church is no accident of history. It isn't true that Jesus died and all he wound up with for his troubles was the stinking Church. It is no consolation prize.

Rather, the Church is the primary instrument through which God's plan of cosmic and eternal salvation is worked out. And it doesn't get any bigger than that.

It was a spur-of-the-moment kind of thing.
-- Anthony Thomas on his run to deliver the football to his wife

**To disdain church involvement is to assert
that God doesn't know what he's doing.**

STRANGE BUT TRUE

Read Philippians 2:1-11.

"And being found in appearance as a man, he humbled himself and became obedient to death – even death on a cross!" (v. 7)

It's strange but true: Michigan head coach Lloyd Carr declared that the biggest play of the 1997 national championship season was an incomplete pass.

George Cantor wrote, "There comes a time in which every good team must fight its way out of a dark place. How well it manages that determines whether it is a great team." For the 1997 Wolverines, the darkest place came at Michigan Stadium on Oct. 18.

At halftime, 15th-ranked Iowa led 5th-ranked Michigan 21-7. In the locker room, Carr asked his players if there was anyone who thought they couldn't come back. "We all knew we could," said linebacker Sam Sword.

So they did. Quarterback Brian Griese hit wide receiver Russell Shaw with a 10-yard pass for one score. Then with 3:11 left in the third, he sneaked in from the 1. The game was tied 21-21.

But Iowa returned the kickoff to the Michigan 26 and got a field goal out of the deal. They led 24-21 deep into the fourth quarter.

With less than seven minutes to play, the Wolverines faced a third and 16 at their own 17. Then came Carr's "biggest play of the season." A pass to wide receiver Tai Streets was incomplete, but an official pulled out a flag. Pass interference and a first down.

WOLVERINES

Just how big was that play? Had Streets made a clean catch, he would have been short of the first down. Given new life by a Hawkeye mistake, the Wolverines used nine plays to score with Griese hitting tight end Jerame Tuman from the 2 with 2:55 left.

That 28-24 score stood up. The Wolverines went 12-0 and won the national title with a season in which -- strangely enough -- an incomplete pass may have been the biggest play.

Life is just strange, isn't it? How else to explain the college bowl situation, tattoos, curling, tofu, and teenagers? Isn't it strange that today we have more ways to stay in touch with each other yet are losing the intimacy of personal contact?

Right at the top, though, of any list of "strange" things about life is God's plan to save us from ourselves. Think a minute about what God did. He could have come roaring down, destroying and blasting everyone whose sinfulness offended him, which, of course, is pretty much all of us. Then he could have brushed off his hands, nodded the divine head, and left a scorched planet in his wake. All in a day's work.

Instead, God came up with a totally novel plan: He would save the world by becoming a human being, letting himself be humiliated, tortured, and killed, thus establishing a kingdom of justice and righteousness that will last forever.

It's a strange way to save the world – but it's true.

It may sound strange, but many champions are made champions by setbacks.

-- Olympic champion Bob Richards

**It's strange but true: God allowed himself
to be killed on a cross to save the world.**

DAY 64

THE GREATEST

Read Mark 9:33-37.

"If anyone wants to be first, he must be the very last, and the servant of all" (v. 35).

It may still rank as the greatest single play in UM women's athletics history, that one swing by freshman Samantha Findlay.

Through seven days in May in 2005, the University of Michigan women's softball team battled back from the brink of defeat to take the national title. They started the Women's College World Series with two shutouts from senior Jennie Ritter against DePaul and Texas. Ritter was a two-time All-America and was twice the university's Female Athlete of the Year.

But the UM women were pushed to the edge of elimination with a 2-0 loss to Tennessee in an 11-inning game that didn't end until 1:21 a.m. Michigan then turned right around and kicked Tennessee out with a 3-2 win. Junior outfielder Stephanie Bercaw hit what turned out to be the game-winning home run in the fourth inning. The win propelled the team into the WCWS finals for the first time against UCLA, the two-time defending champ.

UCLA won the first game of the best two-out-of three series. But before there was Findlay's legendary blast, there was Becky Marx. With Michigan down 2-0 in the fifth inning of the second game, Marx, the team's junior catcher, blasted a two-run homer that ignited a four-run rally and a 5-2 win.

That set up one winner-take-all game.

Described as "running on fumes," Ritter tossed a masterpiece. She threw 119 pitches and allowed only five hits and one run. The teams battled into the tension-filled tenth inning tied at 1. With the national title resting on every pitch, Findlay's legendary blast came with Tiffany Haas and Alessandra Giampaolo on base. Ritter set UCLA down for the 4-1 win and the national title.

Findlay would go on to become one of UM's greatest players, but her greatest moment came her freshman season in the biggest win in the program's history.

We all want to be the greatest. The goal for the Wolverines and their fans every season is the national championship. The competition at work is to be the most productive sales person on the staff or the Teacher of the Year. In other words, we define being the greatest in terms of the struggle for personal success. It's nothing new; Jesus' disciples saw greatness in the same way.

As Jesus illustrated, though, greatness in the Kingdom of God has nothing to do with the secular world's understanding of success. Rather, the greatest are those who channel their ambition toward the furtherance of Christ's kingdom through love and service, rather than their own advancement, which is a complete reversal of status and values as the world sees them.

After all, who could be greater than the person who has Jesus for a brother and God for a father? And that's every one of us.

Samantha Findlay became my hero.
-- Writer Stephanie Wright on Findlay's homer

**To be great for God has nothing to do
with personal advancement and everything to do
with the advancement of Christ's kingdom.**

DAY 65

DREAM WORLD

Read Joshua 3.

"All Israel passed by until the whole nation had completed the crossing on dry ground" (v. 17b).

For Jareth Glanda, every offensive lineman's dream came true: to have the ball in his hands and be rumbling toward the end zone. Only he didn't recover a fumble; he caught a pass.

On Jan. 11, 2011, Brady Hoke was named the 19th head football coach in Michigan history. He led the Wolverines to an 11-2 record in his first season that included an exciting 23-20 overtime win over Virginia Tech in the 2012 Sugar Bowl.

Buried in the game's box score is an apparently routine statistic: Glanda, J., receptions: one, yards: 11. Those eleven yards made "Glanda, J." UM's third-leading receiver for the game.

"Glanda, J." was the Wolverines' long snapper.

Late in the second quarter, Michigan lined up for a field goal attempt. As usual, Glanda, a redshirt sophomore, was the snapper. As the team lined up, sophomore receiver Drew Dileo heard the "Fire Right" call from the sideline; it was a fake.

Dileo dutifully relayed the call down the line of scrimmage. In the noisy Superdome, part of the line didn't hear him.

As a result, the play was a bust. Pressured, Dileo tried to hit tight end Steve Watson but overthrew him. A Tech cornerback got his hands on the ball but then collided with a teammate. The ball caromed off him right into Glanda's hands.

"I was trying to make a couple of blocks and saw the ball go over my head and get deflected," Glanda said. "I came down with it. It was pretty cool."

Not surprisingly, Glanda said he never did "catching drills" at practice. "I snap all the time; that's what I do." Nevertheless, he turned upfield like an experienced wide receiver and rumbled for 11 yards and a Michigan first down in the game's strangest play.

Every lineman's dream.

No matter how tightly or how doggedly we cling to our dreams, devotion to them won't make them a reality. Moreover, the cold truth is that all too often dreams don't come true even when we put forth a mighty effort. The realization of dreams generally results from a head-on collision of persistence and timing.

But what if our dreams don't come true because they're not the same dreams God has for us? That is, they're not good enough and, in many cases, they're not big enough.

God calls us to great achievements because God's dreams for us are greater than our dreams for ourselves. Could the Israelites, wallowing in the misery of slavery, even dream of a land of their own? Could they imagine actually going to such a place?

The fulfillment of such great dreams occurs only when our dreams and God's will for our lives are the same. Our dreams should be worthy of our best – and worthy of God's involvement in making them come true.

This is definitely the biggest catch of my life.
-- Jareth Glanda after the Sugar Bowl

If our dreams are to come true, they must be worthy of God's involvement in them.

DAY 66

FOOD FOR THOUGHT

Read Genesis 9:1-7.

"Everything that lives and moves will be food for you. Just as I gave you the green plants, I now give you everything" *(v. 3).*

For a Wolverine football player struggling to keep his weight down, perhaps driving a potato chip truck during the summer wasn't exactly a great idea.

Jim Brandstatter was a three-year letterman for Michigan at offensive tackle from 1969-71. As a senior he was second-team All-Big Ten. He tells the story that when new head man Bo Schembechler met him for the first time, the coach told him, "You could stand to lose some weight." Thus, the battle began.

Schembechler demanded that none of his players weigh more than 250 pounds, and as Brandstatter moved into his upper-class years, the weight became more of a problem. Each spring the head coach would remind him he had to come back in the fall in shape.

To ensure that, Schembechler monitored his players' summer activities, including their jobs. Offensive line coach Jerry Hanlon did the checking on Brandstatter.

One summer the lineman worked for his brother, who had the distribution rights for a potato chip company. Brandstatter drove a big van around town, marketing and delivering the chips. When Hanlon called to check on his summer job, Brandstatter told him. "The phone went dead silent," he remembered, before Hanlon "used some interesting language. . . . As I recall, the phrase 'fox in a hen house' was used repeatedly."

Dispositions didn't improve when Schembechler asked Hanlon point blank about his lineman's job. Hanlon ruefully told his boss that his starter with a weight problem was driving a potato chip truck for the summer. The coach was not real happy.

Two weeks before he was to report in the fall, Brandstatter left the chip truck and worked out every day. He lost 18 pounds. "I am somewhat impressed," Schembechler said when he saw him.

Belly up to the buffet, boys and girls, for barbecue, some pasta, sirloin steak, grilled chicken, and fried catfish. Rachael Ray's a household name; hamburger joints, pizza parlors, and taco stands lurk on every corner; and we have television channels devoted exclusively to food. We love our chow.

Food is one of God's really good ideas, but consider the complex divine plan that begins with a seed and ends with corn on the cob. The creator of all life devised a system in which living things are sustained and nourished physically through the sacrifice of other living things in a way similar to what Christ underwent to save us spiritually. Whether it's fast food or home-cooked, everything we eat is a gift from God secured through a divine plan in which some plants and animals have given up their lives.

Pausing to give thanks before we dive in is the least we can do.

I was just chunky.
-- Jim Brandstatter on his weight problems as a Wolverine

God created a system that nourishes us
through the sacrifice of other living things;
that's worth a thank-you.

NIGHTFALL

Read Psalm 74:12-23.

"The day is yours, and yours also the night; you established the sun and moon" (v. 16).

Lion Kim made history in 2011 by becoming the first Wolverine golfer to play in the Masters while he was still a student. He got there by playing in the dark.

Kim was an ace as soon as he hit the Michigan campus, playing in every team golf event as a freshman in 2007-08. He was a key part of Wolverine teams that made four straight NCAA appearances. He was a team captain and a multiple All-America.

He earned his invitation to the 2011 Masters by winning the 2010 U.S. Amateur Public Links Championship his junior season. He won it in rather unusual fashion.

Kim played in the final round of match play on July 18, 2010. Or rather, he spent most of the day sitting around, waiting out a seven-hour rain delay. He so dominated his final opponent, however, that he needed to tie or win only one of the last six holes to win the tournament and land an invitation to the Masters.

Kim had one really big problem, however, as his partner and he strolled up to the tee box on the 13th hole. He couldn't see a thing. The long rain delay meant that night fell while the pair was still on the course. "It was pitch dark," Kim recalled.

His opponent and he talked it over. They could play the hole in the dark or come back the next morning. "It had been a long week for both of us," Kim said, so they decided to forge ahead.

Normally, two or three volunteers would be spaced along the hole to spot errant balls. Now they had thirty, "peek[ing] through the oncoming shadows" to help in any way they could. "They had to listen to hear the ball land in order to find where the ball went," Kim said. His opponent and he had to guess how they hit the ball because they couldn't see where it went either.

Kim wound up with an 8-foot putt for the win. Only when the ball disappeared from sight one more time did he know for sure: He was on his way to the Masters.

Except for the golf course, the lighting of our sporting facilities has become commonplace today. With the lighting expertise we have, our night games are played under conditions that are, for all practice purposes, "as bright as day."

It is artificial light, though, man-made, not God-made. Our electric lights can only illumine a portion of God's night; they can never chase it away. The night, like the day, is a gift from God to be enjoyed, to function as a necessary part of our lives. The night is a part of God's plan for creation and is a natural cycle that includes activity and rest.

The world is different at nightfall. Whether we admire a stunning sunset, are dazzled by fireflies, or simply find solace in the descending quiet, the night reminds us of the variety of God's creation and the need the creation has for constant renewal.

Now it's official. I am going to get an invite to the Masters.
-- Lion Kim's thoughts as he won the public links title in the dark

Like the day, night is part of both the beauty and the order of God's creation.

DAY 68

ONE TOUGH COOKIE

Read 2 Corinthians 11:21b-29.

"Besides everything else, I face daily the pressure of my concern for all the churches" (v. 28).

Across the decades, Michigan has fielded some really tough football players. Steve Everitt may still be the toughest of them all.

As a senior in 1992, Everitt enhanced his reputation for toughness by playing on at center despite a dislocated right thumb. He simply snapped the ball with his left hand. The Notre Dame game the previous season, though, had already ensured his enshrinement in the tough guy hall of fame.

On a touchdown run by Ricky Powers in the 24-14 win, Everitt went down. Offensive line coach Les Miles went onto the field to discover that Everitt's jaw was broken in two places so badly that his jaw had separated from his teeth.

As the coach put it, Everitt "was talking without the ability to make words" because "he couldn't operate his tongue with his teeth." What in the world was Everitt trying to say? "Don't worry, I'll be fine. Just take me to the sideline and I'll be fine."

Ignoring Everitt's insistence on getting back into the game, he was taken by ambulance to a hospital. It was not a pleasant trip. "I was trying to tell everyone that I wanted to go back and play," Everitt recalled. After Everitt spent the ride trying to convince the medics that his injury was nothing, he wouldn't let anyone at the hospital knock him out while the game was on TV.

WOLVERINES

The legendary tough man needed three plates to stabilize his jaw. He missed only two games.

During his senior year, Everitt was eating out with his parents when suddenly his mouth started gushing blood. One of the screws holding a plate had backed out into his mouth. After that, his dad always said his son had a screw loose.

You don't have to be a legendary Michigan offensive lineman to be tough. In America today, toughness isn't restricted just to physical accomplishments and brute strength. Going to work every morning even when you feel bad, sticking by your rules for your children in a society that ridicules parental authority, making hard decisions about your aging parents' care often over their objections — you've got to be tough every day just to live honorably, decently, and justly.

Living faithfully requires toughness, too, though in America chances are you won't be imprisoned, stoned, or flogged this week for your faith as Paul was. Still, contemporary society exerts subtle, psychological, daily pressures on you to turn your back on your faith and your values. Popular culture promotes promiscuity, atheism, and gutter language; your children's schools have kicked God out; the corporate culture advocates amorality before the shrine of the almighty dollar.

You have to hang tough to keep the faith.

I don't know whether I was that much tougher than anyone else. I just had a chance to show it more than most guys.
— Steve Everitt on his tough-guy reputation

**Life demands more than mere physical toughness;
you must be spiritually tough too.**

DAY 69

ANGER MANAGEMENT

Read James 1:19-27.

"Everyone should be quick to listen, slow to speak and slow to become angry, for man's anger does not bring about the righteous life that God desires" (vv. 19-20).

A player so angry he smacked Bo Schembechler in the head with a whistle. The coach in return so angry that he chased the player across the practice field. Only part of that was as it seemed.

Greg DenBoer was a three-year letterman for Michigan from 1972-74. A tight end, he started as a senior and caught eight passes, which made him the third-leading receiver on the run-oriented team. He also lettered in track as a shot putter.

All-American running back Rob Lytle, who finished in 1976 as UM's all-time leading rusher, told the story of an angry encounter one day at practice between Schembechler and DenBoer.

Lytle recalled that at the time the team wore wide-mesh jerseys during their summer practices. For some reason, Schembechler was angry about something DenBoer had or had not done. He had a finger in DenBoer's shoulder pad as he barked at his player while the tight end tried unsuccessfully to explain himself.

The coach ended the discussion by ordering, "Go get back in the huddle." That's when the situation went from bad to worse.

As usual, Schembechler's whistle was on a chain around his neck. This time, though, it caught in DenBoer's jersey, and when the two men turned their respective ways, the elastic stretched and then snapped, smacking the coach in the back of his head.

Schembechler erupted in anger, and, as Lytle put it, "The next thing you see is Greg running with Bo screaming after him." As he ran, the head coach was shouting that he never wanted to see DenBoer on his field again.

The players eventually managed to settle Schembechler down and explain to him that DenBoer had not attacked him in anger but that the whistle had gotten stuck in the mesh of the jersey.

Our society today is well aware of anger's destructive power because too many of us don't manage it. Anger is a healthy component of a functional human being until – like other normal emotions such as fear, grief, and worry – it escalates out of control. Anger abounds, of course, when Michigan loses; the problem comes when that anger intensifies from annoyance and disappointment to rage and destructive behavior.

Anger has both practical and spiritual consequences. Its great spiritual danger occurs when anger is "a purely selfish matter and the expression of a merely peevish vexation at unexpected and unwelcome misfortune or frustration" as when Michigan fumbles at the Ohio State five-yard line. It thus interferes with the living of the righteous, Christ-like life God intends for us.

Our own anger, therefore, can incur God's wrath; making God angry can never be anything but a perfectly horrendous idea.

I'll never forget Greg DenBoer running for his life.
-- Rob Lytle

**Anger becomes a problem when it escalates
into rage and interferes with the righteous life
God intends for us.**

DAY 70

WEATHERPROOFED

Read Nahum 1:3-9.

"His way is in the whirlwind and the storm, and clouds are the dust of his feet" (v. 3b).

Michigan once won a game -- and clinched a berth in the Rose Bowl -- without making a first down. Blame it on the weather.

The 1950 Ohio State game is so famous -- or infamous -- that it has its own nickname: The Snow Bowl. The morning of the game a full-fledged blizzard roared into Columbus. The wind blasted everything and everybody at 40 miles an hour, blowing the snow so hard that it came down "horizontally." During the game, the temperature dropped to five above zero.

Scheduled for a 2 p.m. start, the game was delayed for twenty minutes by the difficulty of removing the snow-covered tarpaulin from the field. The ground crew finally had to cut the $3,000 tarp into shreds to remove it. Boy scouts, spectators -- even the referees -- pitched in to help.

The 50,000 or so hardy fans who braved the weather -- many of whom covered their head with a cardboard box as a shield against the merciless wind -- endured one of the strangest games in football history. Michigan didn't make a first down and had only 27 yards of total offense for the game. Ohio State had three first downs. The two teams fumbled a combined ten times, which wasn't too bad considering the conditions. They set an all-time Big-Ten record by punting 45 times, often on first down.

WOLVERINES

Incredibly, Ohio State managed an early field goal, but Michigan won the game on a pair of blocked punts. In the first period, UM blocked a punt that rolled out of the end zone for a safety. Then with only 40 seconds left in the half, UM's Tony Momsen blocked a Buckeye punt and fell on the ball for a touchdown. The PAT was good, and the 9-3 score held up. As the weather worsened, the last half was "just a struggle for survival."

The Wolverines spent New Year's Day in sunny Pasadena.

A thunderstorm washes away your golf game or the family picnic. Lightning knocks out the electricity just as you settle down in front of your TV to watch the Wolverine game. A sudden cold snap ices down your overnight camping trip.

For all our technology and our knowledge, we are still at the mercy of the weather, able only to get a little more advance warning than in the past. The weather answers only to God. Rain and hail will fall where they want to; a blizzard will be totally inconsiderate of something as important as a UM football game.

We stand mute before the awesome power of the weather, but we should be even more awestruck at the power of the one who controls it, a power beyond our imagining. Neither, however, can we imagine the depths of God's love for us, a love that drove him to die on a cross for us.

There were times when you could not see the field from the sidelines and none of us knew what was happening out there.
-- UM linebacker Roger Zatkoff on the 1950 Snow Bowl

The power of the one who controls the weather
is beyond anything we can imagine,
but so is his love for us.

DAY 71

HOME SWEET HOME

Read 2 Corinthians 5:1-10.

"We . . . would prefer to be away from the body and at home with the Lord" (v. 8).

A cowboy in Ann Arbor? A Texan playing hockey? Chris Brown was so far from home he was referred to as "The Lost Cowboy."

When he was 5, Brown watched the 1996 NCAA Hockey Championship, which the Wolverines won. (One of their nine titles, the most in Division I.) He really liked the winged helmets the Michigan skaters wore, so after the game he announced he was going to play hockey for Michigan. Never mind that he was in Flower Mound, Texas, which was not exactly a hockey hotbed and which was more than a thousand miles south of Ann Arbor.

Actually, the notion was not as far-fetched as it might appear. Young Chris's dad had played college hockey, and he had his son on skates from the time he was 2. "I've been on roller blades and skates for as long as I can remember," Brown said.

In Flower Mound, football was the sport of choice, but Chris used other sports only to stay in shape for hockey and to hang out with his friends. As he got better, he simply got too big for Texas.

After his freshman year of high school, he flew to Detroit and a spot on an amateur club team. Fifteen years old, he left everything and everyone he had ever known to live in a culture he knew nothing about with a family he had never met.

Brown was a sophomore when Michigan assistant coach Mel

Pearson offered him a scholarship. Brown excused himself to call his parents. He really had no decision to make; the phone call lasted less than a minute.

In Ann Arbor, Brown wore those cowboy boots, drove a big pick-up truck with Texas license plates, and listened to country music. From 2009-12, he appeared in 125 games and scored 80 points. In 2011-12, as a junior, he scored 29 points in 38 games and was All-CCHA honorable mention.

He also found a second home. A tattoo on his right shoulder depicted two crossed hockey sticks with flags over them. One is a combination Texas-U.S. flag; the other is a Michigan flag.

Home is not necessarily a matter of geography. It may be that place you share with your spouse and your children, whether it's Texas or Michigan. You may feel at home when you return to Ann Arbor, wondering why you were so eager to leave in the first place. Maybe the home you grew up in still feels like an old shoe, a little worn but comfortable and inviting.

God planted that sense of home in us because he is a God of place, and our place is with him. Thus, we may live a few blocks away from our parents and grandparents, or we may relocate every few years, but we will still sometimes feel as though we don't really belong no matter where we are. We don't; our true home is with God in the place Jesus has gone ahead to prepare for us. We are homebodies and we are perpetually homesick.

He's not a typical Michigan kid. He's still a Texan at heart.
— Teammate Kevin Lynch on Chris Brown

We are continually homesick for our real home,
which is with God in Heaven.

ANIMAL MAGNETISM

Read Psalm 139:1-18.

"For you created my inmost being; you knit me together in my mother's womb. I praise you because I am fearfully and wonderfully made" (vv. 13-14).

Michigan remains a program without a live mascot on the sidelines, but that wasn't always the case. The school tried it once; it was an unmitigated disaster.

The problem lay in the mascot itself: the wolverine, which isn't indigenous to Michigan. When UM legend Fielding Yost decided in 1923 he wanted a live mascot at his football games, he couldn't find one. He sent letters to scores of trappers and contacted every letterman he could find. The best he could come up with was a stuffed wolverine from Canada named Biff.

Yost didn't give up, though. In 1927, the Detroit Zoo acquired ten wolverines from Alaska, and Yost struck a deal to have two of them transported to Ann Arbor on game days. They were nicknamed Biff and Bennie and were paraded around the stadium during football games.

"The live wolverines were a disaster," primarily because they were wild animals and were by nature extremely ferocious. For instance, "when Biff was first placed into his cage a week before the [first] game, he snapped a bar in two with his teeth." The animals also grew quite rapidly, and before long, no one was willing to carry them around the stadium in their cage, let alone lead

WOLVERINES

them on a leash. As Yost put it, "It was obvious that the Michigan mascots had designs on the Michigan men toting them, and those designs were by no means friendly."

Yost had to admit that the experiment with the live wolverines was a disappointing failure, and it ended after the 1927 season. Equally a failure was an attempt in the 1980s to have a costumed mascot at the games. Willy the Wolverine was so unpopular he was eventually banned from the stadium in the fall of 1989.

Wild animals elicit our awe and our respect. Nothing enlivens a trip more than glimpsing turkeys, bears, or deer in the wild. Admit it: You go along with the kids' trip to the zoo because you think it's a cool place too. All that variety of life is mind-boggling. Who could conceive of a wolverine, a walrus, a moose, or a prairie dog? Who could possibly have that rich an imagination?

But the next time you're in a crowd, look around at the parade of faces. Who could come up with the idea for all those different people? For that matter, who could ever imagine something like you? You are unique, a masterpiece who will never be duplicated.

The master creator, God Almighty, is behind it all. He thought of you and brought you into being. If you had a manufacturer's label, it might say, "Lovingly, fearfully, and wonderfully handmade in Heaven by #1 -- God."

[Fielding] Yost had not accounted for the rapid growth or the ferocity of the animals.
    -- National Geographic *on problems with the live UM mascots*

You may consider some painting or a magnificent animal a work of art, but the real masterpiece is you.

DAY 73

SUPERSTITION

Read Isaiah 2:6-16.

"They are full of superstitions from the East; . . . they bow down to the work of their hands" (vv. 6b, 8b).

From folding their napkins a certain way to tossing the quarterback into the air, the Wolverines of 2011 kept to their pregame superstitions.

For instance, if you looked closely at linebacker J.B. Fitzgerald when he took the field for a game (2008-11), you may have been perceptive enough to notice something peculiar about his eye black. It wasn't eye black; it was shoe polish. He picked up that superstition when he was in the second grade and noticed older players wearing eye black. He asked his dad to get him some. Instead, his father handed him a can of black shoe polish; Fitzgerald wore it every game after that.

Junior quarterback Denard Robinson had a rather strange pregame superstition. He insisted that offensive tackle Taylor Lewman throw him into the air. Fortunately, the 6-8, 302-lb. lineman never failed to catch his field general. Twice, though, they forgot the toss; it was the only times the Wolverines lost all season.

Robinson shared a pregame ritual with his head coach, Brady Hoke: The two didn't eat on game days. Only once all season did Hoke give in and chow down; that was before the Notre Dame game, which didn't kick off until 8 p.m.

The special teams crowd all folded their napkins a certain way after dinner the night before a game. Junior safety Jordan Kovacs always wore a particular shoe the night before the games.

Fitzgerald explained that superstitions are so widespread because "that's what makes you feel comfortable in the game and ready to go out and play."

Freshman cornerback Blake Countess had the most solid pre-game ritual of all. Before every game, he always made sure he took time off by himself to pray.

Superstitions – such as wearing shoe polish -- can be quite benign. Nothing in the Bible warns us about the dangers inherent in folding our napkins in a particular manner.

God is quite concerned, however, about superstition of a more serious nature such as using the occult to predict the future. Its danger for us is that we allow something other than God to take precedence in our lives; we in effect worship idols.

While most of us scoff at palm readers and psychics, we nevertheless risk being idol worshippers of a different sort. Just watch the frenzied reaction of fans when a movie star or a star football player shows up. Or consider how we often compromise what we know is right merely to save face or to gain favor in the workplace.

Superstition is the stuff of nonsense. Idol worshipping, however, is as real for us today as it was for the Israelites. It is also just as dangerous.

It's football, and a lot of superstition is wrapped up into the game.
-- Senior linebacker J.B. Fitzgerald in 2011

**Superstition in the form of idol worship
is alive and well today, occurring anytime
we venerate anything other than God.**

DAY 74

NAME DROPPING

Read Exodus 3:13-20.

"God said to Moses, 'I AM WHO I AM. This is what you are to say to the Israelites: 'I AM has sent me to you'" (v. 14).

The generation gap between coach and players was never revealed more starkly that when Bo Schembechler slapped what he thought was a clever nickname on one of his plays.

In the spring of 1969, Schembechler was the new man on the Michigan campus, and he brought with him a new offense, a new defense, and a new terminology. Perhaps most famous as the long-time color commentator on the Michigan football radio broadcasts, Jim Brandstatter was an offensive tackle on Schembechler's first teams (1969-71). He tells the story of one meeting under the stands of the baseball stadium when the new head man vigorously introduced his new offensive playbook to his players.

As the coach diagrammed feverishly on a blackboard, he said, "OK, now we get to our reverse. We call it a 'Sally.'" Brandstatter recalled that the guys -- all between 18 and 21 -- looked around at each other all dazed and confused. When Schembechler turned around, he sensed he'd lost his team.

He quickly realized that these youngsters had no clue about "Sally." He explained that the play was named after Sally Rand, a stripper who had a gimmick that separated her from other Burlesque queens: She covered herself up with feathered fans. The coach said that the audience knew she was naked underneath, but she teased them with the feathers.

"That's why we call this play a 'Sally,'" he said. "Its our naked reverse." The whole room lapsed into one massive groan, except for Schembechler, who just stood there with a playful grin on his face. "The fact was," Brandstatter said, "we did call it a 'Sally.'" He added, "We made big plays with the 'Sally' all the time."

Nicknames such as the "Sally" are not slapped haphazardly upon individuals or even football plays but reflect perceptions about the person or object named. Proper names do that also.

Nowhere throughout history has this concept been more prevalent than in the Bible, where a name is not a mere label but is an expression of the essential nature of the named one. That is, a person's name reveals his or her character. Even God shares this concept; to know the name of God is to know God as he has chosen to reveal himself to us.

What does your name say about you? Honest, trustworthy, a seeker of the truth and a person of God? Or does the mention of your name cause your coworkers to whisper snide remarks, your neighbors to roll their eyes, or your friends to start making allowances for you?

Most importantly, what does your name say about you to God? He, too, knows you by name.

You want to run the Sally?
-- Bo Schembechler to assistant Jerry Hanlon in the press box

Live so that your name evokes positive
associations by people you know,
by the public, and by God.

DAY 75

GOAL ORIENTED

Read 1 Peter 1:3-12.

"For you are receiving the goal of your faith, the salvation of your souls" (v. 9).

When Albert Wistert told a reporter his goal was to be an All-America at Michigan, the newsman couldn't believe it. After all, Wistert didn't even play high school football.

Wistert's father, a Chicago police sergeant, was shot and killed when Albert was 6 years old, leaving a widow with six children. Not surprisingly, money was always a real problem in the household. Mom refused to let her boys play football because if they got hurt, she wouldn't have enough money to pay the medical bills. Wistert got in some football by playing for a Chicago parks team, which didn't require his mother's permission. He admitted, though, "I was pretty green as far as football was concerned."

Albert's older brother, Francis or "Whitey," did play some high school football, had subsequently been invited to Michigan by a friend, and had become an All-America there. He then joined the Michigan coaching staff, so it was, as Albert put it, "only natural" that he follow his brother to Michigan.

When Albert arrived in Ann Arbor, he was so unschooled in the finer points of the game that head coach Fritz Crisler "despaired of awkward Al ever becoming a football player." "Awkward Al" was confident, though, letting that reporter in on his goal.

Albert broke his ankle in 1939 and sat out the season to keep the year of eligibility. When he returned to the field, "the clumsiness was gone, replaced by astonishing strength and speed."

He became an immediate starter at tackle in 1940 and was All-Western Conference three years in a row. He even realized every down lineman's dream: He got to carry the ball in a game. His chance came against Northwestern in 1941, a 14-7 UM win. On the play he broke a wrist and his nose. "I decided no more of that," Wistert said.

And about that goal the reporter thought was so ridiculous? In 1942, Albert joined his older brother Francis as an All-America.

What are your goals for your life? Have you ever thought them out? Or do you just shuffle along living for your paycheck and any fun you can find instead of pursuing some greater purpose?

Now try this one: What is the goal of your faith life? You go to church to worship God. You read the Bible and study God's word to learn about God and how God wants you to live. But what is it you hope to achieve? What is all that stuff about? For what purpose do you believe that Jesus Christ is God's son?

The answer is actually quite simple: The goal of your faith life is your salvation, and this is the only goal in life that matters. Nothing you will ever seek is as important or as eternal as getting into Heaven and making sure that everybody you know and love will be there too one day.

I want to be an All-American like my brother, Whitey.
-- Albert Wistert on his goals for his football career

**The most important goal of your life
is to get to Heaven and to help as many people
as you can to get there one day too.**

DAY 76

THE LIST

Read Exodus 20:1-17.

*"God spoke all these words: 'I am the Lord your God . . . .
You shall have no other gods before me'" (vv. 1, 3).*

The first-ever national title for a UM women's program tops one writer's list of the school's ten greatest sports moments of the decade of the 2000s.

On Jan. 13, 2010, John U. Bacon assembled his list of "the greatest, most memorable, most inspiring moments of the '00s" for Michigan fans. No. 1 on the list was the field hockey team's 2-0 win over Maryland on Nov. 18, 2001, that won the school's first national title for a woman's program. (See Devotion No. 51.)

No. 2 on Bacon's list was the second UM women's national title, that of the 2005 softball team, which upset perennial powerhouse UCLA 4-1 in ten innings for the title. (See Devotion No. 64.)

Next up was Kevin Porter's winning the Hobey Baker Award, college hockey's equivalent of the Heisman, in 2008.

Bacon's fourth top moment of the decade was the 2001 season of the women's gymnastics team, which missed the national title by 0.125. Freshman Elise Ray tied as the national all-around champ on her way to becoming the most decorated UM athlete ever.

Head football coach Lloyd Carr's exit on Jan. 1, 2008, was next on Bacon's list. The Wolverines upset 12th-ranked Florida 41-35 in the Capital One Bowl and gave their head man a ride on their shoulders in celebration.

WOLVERINES

No. 6 was Tiffany Ofili's five NCAA titles in the hurdles. Next was Steve Luke's national title in 2009. Luke went 32-0 as a senior wrestler. No. 8 was the performance of UM athletes in the 2000 Sydney Olympics. Fifteen athletes participated; eight won medals.

A pair of returns rounded out Bacon's list: The return of the UM men's basketball team to the NCAA tournament in 2009 and the return of the baseball program to prominence starting in 2006.

For Wolverine fans, these are indeed ten to remember.

You've got your list and you're ready to go: a gallon of paint and a water hose from the hardware store; chips, peanuts, and sodas from the grocery store for watching tonight's football game with your buddies; the tickets for the band concert. Your list helps you remember.

God also made a list once of things he wanted you to remember; it's called the Ten Commandments. Just as your list reminds you to do something, so does God's list remind you of how you are to act in your dealings with other people and with him.

A life dedicated to Jesus is a life devoted to relationships, and God's list emphasizes that the social life and the spiritual life of the faithful cannot be sundered. God's relationship to you is one of unceasing, unqualified love, and you are to mirror that divine love in your relationships with others. In case you forget, you have a list.

Society today treats the Ten Commandments as if they were the ten suggestions. Never compromise on right or wrong.
-- College baseball coach Gordie Gillespie

God's list is a set of instructions on how you are to conduct yourself with other people and with him.

DAY 77

STAR POWER

Read Luke 10:1-3, 17-20.

"The Lord appointed seventy-two others and sent them two by two ahead of him to every town and place where he was about to go" (v. 1).

With his team off to a horrendous start, Wolverine head coach Lloyd Carr called in some real star power to inspire his players.

The 2007 team, Carr's last, won nine games, finished second in the Big Ten, and whipped Florida 41-35 in the Capital One Bowl. At one stretch, they won eight straight games, including defeats of Penn State, Illinois, and Michigan State.

During the drive to the national title in 1997, Carr had demonstrated his genius for motivating his team by bringing in a well-known mountain climber and author who had tackled Mount Everest. In 2007, the head Wolverine pulled in an even bigger gun: Academy-Award winning actor Russell Crowe.

The Wolverines were 0-2 with Notre Dame up next when Carr got a call from Crowe. The two had forged a friendship when Carr -- up to his old motivational tactics -- showed his 2006 team clips of Crowe's film *Cinderella Man*. "I was really touched that he was using it," Crowe said. The two met, and in May 2007 Carr flew to Australia to speak to Crowe's rugby team.

When Crowe saw the Wolverines struggling, he figured he'd return the favor. "My friend was in a bit of pain, so I thought I'd just take his mind off things," the movie star explained. Carr didn't hesitate to accept his offer to talk to the team.

Thus, on Sept. 15, Russell Crowe gave the pre-game speech to the star-struck Wolverines. He was reticent about what he said, but it must have helped. Michigan whipped Notre Dame 38-0.

Crowe joined the Wolverines on the sideline for the game, even grabbing the Go Blue banner during the team's entrance onto the field. He admitted he was a little awed by the crowd; the largest audience his rugby team had ever had was 34,500.

Football teams are like movies in that they may have a star such as Russell Crowe but the star would be nothing without the supporting cast. It's the same in any organization, whether it's a private company, a government bureaucracy, a military unit, or just about any other team of people with a common goal.

That includes the team known as a church. It may have its "star" in the preacher, who is – like the quarterback or the company CEO – the most visible representative of the team. Preachers are, after all, God's paid, trained professionals.

But when Jesus assembled a team of seventy-two folks, he didn't have anybody on the payroll or any seminary graduates. All he had were no-names who loved him. And nothing has changed. God's church still depends on those whose only pay is the satisfaction of serving and whose only qualification is their love for God. God's church needs you.

It was an incredible privilege to be part of being here today.
– Russell Crowe on the Notre Dame game of 2007

Yes, the church needs its professional clergy,
but it also needs those who serve as volunteers
because they love God; the church needs you.

UNBELIEVABLE!

Read Hebrews 3:1-12.

"See to it, brothers, that none of you has a sinful, unbelieving heart that turns away from the living God" *(v. 12).*

What Michigan did on Nov. 8, 1997, was simply unbelievable.

Networks billed it as Judgment Day: 4th-ranked Michigan vs. 3rd-ranked Penn State. The experts liked Penn State for several reasons, most importantly home field, proven coach, good team. Also, Penn State had whipped Michigan three straight times; the last two years the game had not been close. "We don't have to prepare for them; they have to prepare for us," declared the Penn State fullback. He wasn't arrogant, just honest. Even UM quarterback Brian Griese agreed. "We have to respect them," he admitted. "We've given them no reason to respect us."

That all changed in a hurry. Unbelievable as it sounds, Penn State ran three plays, and the game for all practical purposes was over.

After Michigan kicked a field goal, the Nittany Lions lined confidently up at their 25. They tried a pass off a fake reverse, the idea being to use Michigan's aggressive defense against itself. The quarterback never even got the chance to turn out of the reverse before senior defensive end Glen Steele, a first-team All America that season, had him for a ten-yard loss. After a failed running play, Penn State tried a dropback pass. This time Juaquin Feazell got him. Seven yard loss.

Penn State never recovered as Michigan's defense blew their offense to smithereens. By halftime it was 24-0, the biggest lead ever run up on a Joe Paterno team in Happy Valley. The final was 34-8 with Penn State scoring a meaningless touchdown late.

After that unbelievable performance, the pollsters believed. On Sunday, Michigan jumped up to number one in the rankings.

Much of what taxes the limits of our belief system has little effect on our lives. Maybe we don't believe in UFOs, honest politicians, aluminum baseball bats, Sasquatch, or the viability of electric cars. A healthy dose of skepticism is a natural defense mechanism that helps protect us in a world that all too often has designs on taking advantage of us.

That's not the case, however, when Jesus and God are part of the mix. Quite unbelievably, we often hear people blithely assert they don't believe in God. Or brazenly declare they believe in God but don't believe Jesus was anything but a good man and a great teacher.

At this point, unbelief becomes dangerous because God doesn't fool around with scoffers. He locks them out of the Promised Land, which isn't a country in the Middle East but Heaven itself.

Given that scenario, it's downright unbelievable that anyone would not believe.

Any student who couldn't make the trip to State College was in front of a television set. And they couldn't believe what they were seeing.
-- George Cantor on the '97 Penn State game

Perhaps nothing is as unbelievable as that some people insist on not believing in God or his son.

DAY 79

GETTING ALONG

Read Romans 14:13-23.

"For the kingdom of God is not a matter of eating and drinking, but of righteousness, peace and joy in the Holy Spirit (v. 17).

The Wolverine offensive line was once in such violent disagreement with the coaches that the players pulled a mutiny and refused to go back onto the field unless their demands were met.

Undefeated and ranked second in the country, the Buckeyes were favored in The Big Game of 1995. The Wolverines figured, though, they could run the ball behind the offensive line. For the season, the team averaged more than 200 yards rushing per game.

Sure enough, Michigan opened the game with a little drive on the ground. Then the coaches called for a pass, which was intercepted. The linemen were not at all happy.

The coaches apologized and promised they would stick with the run. Sure enough, the Wolverines started another drive, again on the ground. Sure enough, the coaches called a pass. And sure enough, the pass was intercepted. Again, the line grumbled at the coaches as they disgustedly headed back to the bench.

Wolverine running back Tshimanga Biakabutuka, "Tim" to the fans, had 197 yards in the first half, but because of the passes, Michigan led only 10-9. Incredibly, it happened again. In the third quarter, an interception halted another Michigan drive.

This time the line had had enough. "There was an attempted

coup," said All-American center Rod Payne. In fact, it was a full-fledged coup. The hacked-off offensive line told the coaches they weren't going back into the game if they threw another pass. "Believe me, it was a pretty heated conversation," Payne said.

The coaches got the message. Michigan rushed for more than 400 yards with Biakabutuka getting an astounding 313 yards. Revolution and all, the Wolverines won 31-23.

The only time folks haven't disagreed among themselves was when Adam roamed the garden alone. Since then – well, we just can't seem to get along.

That includes Christians, who have never exactly been role models for peaceful coexistence among themselves. Not only does the greater body of Christ always seem to be spatting and feuding, but discord within individual churches is so common-place that God uses church splits to grow his kingdom.

Why can't Christians get along? Perhaps it's because we take our faith so seriously, which is a good thing. But perhaps also, it's because – as Paul warned – we can't separate the important stuff from the trivial.

Following Christ is about achieving righteousness, joy, and peace, not about following arcane, arbitrary prescriptions for daily living or even worship. All too often we don't get along because the rules and traditions we espouse -- and not Christ's love – govern our hearts and our faith.

It was a mutiny from the offensive line.
-- All-American center Rod Payne on the '95 OSU game

Christians will never get along as long as we worry about and harp on things that we shouldn't.

DAY 80

POP THE QUESTION

Read Matthew 16:13-17.

"'But what about you?' he asked. 'Who do you say I am?'" (v. 15)

Tom Goss had a question that he felt certainly merited a serious reply: "Where's my arm?"

Goss was a defensive lineman who later became Michigan's ninth athletic director. As a senior in 1968 on Bump Elliott's last team, he was named a first-team All-Big Ten defensive end.

During the Minnesota game of 1967, Goss was double-teamed on a play. One of the Gopher linemen grabbed him by the arm and pulled down at the same time, unfortunately, as Goss yanked his arm up. The result was an audible "Pop!"

Goss landed flat on his back and had time to look around and notice that linebacker Frank Nunley had been knocked unconscious on the play. Only then did Goss notice something much more disturbing: He couldn't feel his forearm.

When the trainers arrived, he had a very pointed question for them that demanded an immediate answer. "Where's my arm?" he asked, quite understandably concerned. Only then did he get the answer to his question, spotting his arm, which was still quite attached where it should be, though his elbow was sitting off to one side where it probably shouldn't have been.

As Goss later learned, his elbow had been pulled out of its socket. As he also learned once the initial shock wore off, "That was the most painful experience in my life."

The treatment was routine and swift. He trotted to the sideline where the trainers popped the elbow back into place and rewarded him with a pair of painkillers. "That was that," Goss recalled. "That's when men were *tough*."

Life is an ongoing search for answers, and thus whether our life is lived richly or is wasted is largely determined by both the quality and the quantity of the answers we find. Life is indeed one question after another. What's for dinner? Can we afford a new car? What kind of team will Michigan have this season? And in Tom Goss' case, "Where's my arm?"

But we also continuously seek answers to questions at another, more crucial level. What will I do with my life? Why am I here? Why does God allow suffering and tragedy?

An aspect of wisdom is reconciling ourselves to and being comfortable with the fact that we will never know all of the answers. Equally wise is the realization that the answers to life's more momentous questions lie within us, not beyond us.

One question overrides all others, the one Jesus asked Peter: "Who do you say I am?" Peter gave the one and only correct answer: "You are the Son of the Living God." How you answer that question is really the only one that matters, since it decides not just how you spend your life but how you spend eternity.

Age is a question of mind over matter. If you don't mind, it doesn't matter.

-- Leroy 'Satchel' Paige

Only one question in life determines your eternal fate: Who do you say Jesus is?

DAY 81

JUST AMAZING!

Read: Luke 4:31-36.

"All the people were amazed and said to each other, 'What is this teaching? With authority and power he gives orders to evil spirits and they come out!'" (v. 36)

What the 2010 Wolverine baseball team did against Northwestern was so amazing that ESPN featured it on SportsCenter.

The Wolverines finished the 2010 season with a 35-22 record and a second-place finish in the Big Ten. In the greater scheme of a program that has won two national championships (1953 and 1962), the 2010 season wasn't particularly spectacular -- except for one amazing afternoon.

On Sunday, May 16, at Ray Fisher Stadium, Michigan came to bat in the bottom of the third inning trailing Northwestern by a debilitating 14-0 score. Back-to-back singles to start the inning didn't seem like much, but junior leftfielder Ryan LaMarre followed up with a home run to put a little life into the team. They scored three more to ease their way back into the game at 14-6.

While Northwestern suddenly couldn't score, sophomore third baseman John Lorenz led off the fifth with a home run. Freshman shortstop Derek Dennis chased another run home with a ground ball, and freshman centerfielder Patrick Biondi drove a pair in with a single. Lorenz' single in the sixth brought in another run.

Heading into the seventh inning, Michigan trailed only 14-10, and with Matt Miller on the mound throwing zeroes, an amazing comeback seemed imminently possible. It happened.

Catcher Chris Berset's two-run homer in the seventh made it 14-12. Then with two outs in the bottom of the ninth on an 0-2 count, Berset did the most amazing thing. With Biondi on second, he blasted his second homer of the game. The game was tied at 14.

Senior first baseman Mike Dufek completed the amazing comeback when he launched a solo shot in the 10th. UM won 15-14.

The word amazing defines the limits of what you believe to be plausible or usual. The Grand Canyon, the birth of your children, those last-second UM wins or comebacks -- they're just amazing! You've never seen anything like that before!

Some people in Galilee felt the same way when they encountered Jesus. Jesus amazed them with the authority of his teaching, and he wowed them with his power over spirit beings. People everywhere just couldn't quit talking about him.

It would have been amazing had they not been amazed. They were, after all, witnesses to the most amazing spectacle in the history of the world: God himself was right there among them walking, talking, teaching, preaching, and healing.

Their amazement must be a part of your life too because Jesus still lives. The almighty, omnipotent God of the universe seeks to spend time with you every day – because he loves you. Amazing!

It's amazing. Some of the greatest characteristics of being a winning football player are the same ones it's true of to be a Christian man.
-- Bobby Bowden

Everything about God is amazing,
but perhaps most amazing of all is that
he loves us and desires our company.

DAY 82

FEAR FACTOR

Read Matthew 14:22-33.

"[The disciples] cried out in fear. But Jesus immediately said to them: 'Take courage! It is I. Don't be afraid'" (vv. 26-27).

Butch Woolfolk was so scared he couldn't hear anything, so he just did what he was told -- in front of more than 100,000 people who were watching every move he made.

From 1978-81, Woolfolk set school records for most rushing attempts (718) and most yards rushing (3,861). He led the team in rushing three straight seasons. His 92-yard run against Wisconsin in 1979 is the longest touchdown run in Wolverine history. He was the team MVP in '81 and the MVP of the '81 Rose Bowl.

In 1978, the freshman tailback expected to be redshirted. Injuries to Harlan Huckleby and Russell Davis changed all that, however, and he was thrust into the starting lineup for the Oct. 28 home game against Minnesota. He was so unknown his name wasn't even in the game program.

The first time Woolfolk trotted onto the field "I was really scared. . . . I have to tell you, I couldn't hear anything." If quarterback Rick Leach had changed the play, "I would have been lost."

Woolfolk admitted he was green. "I didn't know what I was doing," he said. He just did what Leach and the older guys told him to do. They helped out by taking the time to calm him down in the huddle before each play. "I was really kind of numb about the whole thing," Woolfolk said.

The youngster could certainly be excused for being just slightly short of terrified. He was 18 years old, he had expected to spend the year gaining some maturity, and here he was on the field in The Big House in front of a sellout crowd.

Woolfolk calmed his fears long enough to rush for 120 yards and a touchdown on 22 carries. Behind their green and scared tailback, the Wolverines buried Minnesota 42-10.

Some fears are universal; others are particular. Speaking to the Rotary Club may require a heavy dose of antiperspirant. Elevator walls may feel as though they're closing in on you. And don't even get started on being in the dark with spiders and snakes during a thunderstorm.

We all live in fear, and God knows this. Dozens of passages in the Bible urge us not to be afraid. God isn't telling us to lose our wariness of oncoming cars or big dogs with nasty dispositions; this is a helpful fear God instilled in us for protection. What God does wish driven from our lives is a spirit of fear that dominates us, that makes our lives miserable and keeps us from doing what we should, such as sharing our faith. In commanding that we not be afraid, God reminds us that when we trust completely in him, we find peace that calms our fears.

It got to me when I went through the tunnel for the first time. It was really, really scary.

-- Butch Woolfolk

**You have your own peculiar set of fears,
but they should never paralyze you
because God is greater than anything you fear.**

| DAY 83 | **LOVE OF YOUR LIFE** |

Read 1 John 4:7-21.

"Whoever does not love does not know God, because God is love" (v. 8).

With all his heart, Bob Chappuis wanted one teenage romance to stay hot and heavy.

In 1942, Chappuis was a sophomore tailback for Michigan; he was called to active duty in January 1943. In February 1945, he was part of a B-25 crew that was shot down over Italy. Chappuis and two other crew members were found by a local partisan who sheltered them in a pink stucco house two doors down from the local headquarters of the German army.

Despite that extremely unfortunate geography, the house was an ideal place in which to hide. The mother and her two daughters were seamstresses, so the constant traffic provided cover for the activity of the partisans. The father ran a local food market, so the Americans had plenty to eat without any suspicion being raised.

The airmen had to stay in one upstairs bedroom and sleep on two tiny beds pushed together. Their room was both a refuge and a prison. Boredom and anxiety were problems, both exacerbated by their ignorance about how long they would have to hide.

One night at dinner, they were surprised by a visit from one of the girls' boyfriends, a Fascist. When he asked who the three men were, his sweetheart told him the truth. He replied that he had to turn them in. The teenager responded, "Go ahead. They will be taken prisoner, but my family and I will be shot." Love won out, and the boy didn't turn the Americans in.

When the war ended a few weeks later, Chappuis returned to Michigan for the fall semester of 1946. Despite weight loss from his confinement, he broke the league record for total offense. In 1947, he led Michigan to an undefeated season, was a consensus All-America, and finished second in the Heisman voting.

Your heart rate accelerates, your mouth runs dry, your blood pressure jumps, your vision blurs, and you start stammering. Either you've got the flu or the one you're in love with just walked into the room and smiled at you. Fortunately, if the attraction is based on more than hormones and eye candy, the feverish frenzy that characterizes newfound love matures into a deeper and more meaningful affection. If it didn't, we'd probably die from exhaustion, stroke, heart failure, or a combination thereof.

We pursue true love with a desperation and a ferocity that is unmatched by any other desire. Ultimately, the Christian life is about that same search, about falling in love and becoming a partner in a deep-seated, satisfying, ever-growing and ever-deepening relationship. The Christian life is all about loving so fiercely and so completely that love is not something we're in but something we are. The object of our love is the greatest and most faithful lover of them all: God.

I don't think I've ever wanted a relationship to succeed more than that one.
— *Bob Chappuis on the Italian teenagers' romance*

God is head-over-heels in love with you;
like any lover, he wants you to return the love.

DAY 84

IN GOD'S OWN TIME

Read James 5:7-12.

"Be patient, then, brothers, until the Lord's coming" (v. 7).

David Harris was so impatient that when he was at Michigan he came back too soon from an injury. That's no surprise considering he showed the same trait as a child.

Harris was always impatient when it came to football. He got his first chance to play when he was 8 -- and was too heavy. The coaches compromised by letting him play offense but not defense.

In the fifth grade, Harris was eight pounds over the weight limit, so he took matters into his own hands. When his mother came home that day, she found her son encased in Saran Wrap from his neck to his toes. After she cut him loose, mom and dad decided to move him up to the senior team.

Again, all the impatient Harris wanted to do was get onto the field, but in the ninth grade he ran into another obstacle. He was so good that he practiced with the varsity. Harris decided to have none of that. Two days before the season started, he asked the coaches to move him down to JV; he didn't want to waste the whole season sitting on the bench.

Harris' impatience revealed itself at Michigan, too. He was redshirted in 2002, and in the second game of 2003, he tore his left ACL. A year after the injury, he returned to the field, but it was too soon. In his first-ever start, against Iowa, the injured leg locked up. He couldn't play the following week, against Indiana.

His mother advised him to "just take it easy" and not rush his recovery too fast. Harris quelled his impatience enough to sit out four more games before finally hitting the field again. In 2005, his comeback was complete. From his linebacking spot, he led the Wolverines in tackles. In 2006, he was All-Big Ten and a second-team All-America. His patience paid off when he was drafted in 2007 in the second round by the New York Jets.

Have you ever left a restaurant because the server didn't take your order quickly enough? Complained at your doctor's office about how long you had to wait? Wondered how much longer a sermon was going to last?

It isn't just the machinations of the world with which we're impatient; we want God to move at our pace, not his. For instance, how often have you prayed and expected – indeed, demanded – an immediate answer from God? And aren't Christians the world over impatient for the glorious day when Jesus will return and set everything right? We're in a hurry but God obviously isn't.

As rare as it seems to be, patience is nevertheless included among the likes of gentleness, humility, kindness, and compassion as attributes of a Christian.

God expects us to be patient. He knows what he's doing, he is in control, and his will shall be done. On his schedule, not ours.

You don't give your body time to heal, you can do more damage to it than was originally done.
> *-- David Harris' mother urging him to be patient*

**God moves in his own time, so often we must wait
for him to act, remaining faithful and patient.**

DAY 85

BELIEVE IT

Read John 3:16-21.

*"For God so loved the world that He gave His only
begotten Son, that whoever believes in Him should not
perish but have everlasting life" (v. 16 NKJV).*

Michigan head basketball coach John Beilein stopped on his
way to the locker room at halftime to look up at the scoreboard.
He just couldn't believe what had just happened to his team.

On Jan. 7, 2009, the 11-3 Wolverines hit the road to Blooming-
ton to take on a woeful Indiana team. The Hoosiers were 5-8 with
a squad that included nine freshmen and ranked dead last in the
Big Ten in more than half of the major statistical categories.

As expected, one of the teams was miserable the first half. Unex-
pectedly, the team was Michigan. "We played a terrible first half,"
declared senior guard and team captain C.J. Lee. The Wolverines
shot 25 per cent in the half, were only 3-for-18 from behind the
arc, and consistently let Indiana drive for layups. One Michigan
layup attempt wound up sailing over the backboard.

As a result, Indiana led 39-22 at halftime. At the buzzer, Beilein
"grabbed his jacket, picked up his water, put his head down" and
headed for the locker room. He paused long enough to stare at the
scoreboard in disbelief.

"We didn't quit," Beilein said. No, they didn't. The Wolverines
played a whole lot better in the last half, which was believable. They
probably couldn't have played much worse.

WOLVERINES

But they still trailed by six with less than a minute left. Sophomore Manny Harris hit a three-pointer, but Indiana beat UM's press, leaving Lee to defend a 2-on-1 fast break. He did, stealing the ball. Redshirt freshman Laval Lucas-Perry, who had a game-high 18 points, nailed a trey to tie the game and send it into overtime, which Michigan dominated for a 72-66 win.

After a first half Beilein found difficult to believe, the Wolverines pulled off a rally and a win that was also hard to believe.

What we believe underscores everything about our lives. Our politics. How we raise our children. How we treat other people. Whether we respect others, their property and their lives.

Often, competing belief systems clamor for our attention; we all know persons – maybe friends and family members – who lost Christianity in the shuffle and the hubbub. We turn aside from believing in Christ at our peril, however, because the heart and soul, the very essence of Christianity, is belief.

That is, believing that this man named Jesus is the very Son of God and that it is through him – and only through him – that we can find forgiveness and salvation that will reserve a place for us with God.

But believing in Jesus is more than simply acknowledging intellectually that he is God. Even the demons who serve Satan know that. Rather, it is belief so deep that we entrust our lives and our eternity to Christ. We live like we believe it – because we do.

If you can believe it, the mind can achieve it.
-- Pro football hall-of-famer Ronnie Lott

**Believe it: Jesus is the way – and the only way
– to eternal life with God.**

DAY 86

WATER POWER

Read Acts 10:34-48.

"Can anyone keep these people from being baptized with water? They have received the Holy Spirit just as we have" (v. 47).

If you want it, you'll have to come up and win it." With that brusque challenge, the battle for one of college football's oldest and oddest trophies was launched.

The Michigan-Minnesota game of Oct. 31, 1903 was a meeting of powerhouses. The Golden Gophers were unbeaten and would finish the season 14-0-1. The Wolverines of the legendary Fielding Yost had won twenty-eight straight games.

After his team arrived in Minneapolis, Yost realized he didn't have anything to hold the players' drinking water. Since he didn't trust his opponents across the way to provide his boys with pure water, he sent team manager Tommy Roberts to a local store to buy a container. What Roberts came back with was a 15-pound, 5-gallon water jug that cost the team 30 cents. It became known as the Little Brown Jug.

When Minnesota scored in the fourth quarter to tie the game 6-6, Gopher fans "celebrated as though they had just won the national championship." They stormed the field and refused to leave even though the game wasn't over. Officials had no choice but to call the game, and the Michigan players hurried to leave the field and the melee. In their haste, they left the jug behind.

Minnesota equipment manager Oscar Munson found the jug the next day and turned it over to the Gophers' athletic director. Inspired by his team's great play, the AD inscribed on the jug, "Michigan Jug. Captured by Oscar October 31, 1903."

Yost later wrote to the athletic director and asked for the jug's return. His replay was, "If you want it, you'll have to come up and win it." The Wolverines had to wait until 1909 to go up there and win it and thereby officially begin the battle for the Little Brown Jug because that's when the teams played next. UM won 15-6.

Children's wading pools and swimming pools in the backyard. Fishing, boating, skiing, and swimming at a lake. Sun, sand, and surf at the beach. Even a Little Brown Jug. If there's any water around, we'll probably be in it, on it, or near it. If there's not any at hand, we'll build a dam and create our own.

We love the wet stuff for its recreational uses, but water first and foremost is about its absolute necessity to support and maintain life. From its earliest days, the Christian church appropriated water as an image of life through the ritual of baptism. Since the time of the arrival of the Holy Spirit at Pentecost, baptism with water has been the symbol of entry into the Christian community. It is water that marks a person as belonging to Jesus. It is through water that a person proclaims that Jesus is his Lord.

There's something in the water, all right. There is life.

The rivalry has been a lopsided one since the schools began playing annually in 1929.
– Game Day: Michigan Football *on the battle for the Little Brown Jug*

There is life in the water:
physical life and spiritual life.

DAY 87

TEARS IN HEAVEN

Read Revelation 21:1-8.

"[God] will wipe every tear from their eyes. There will be
no more death or mourning or crying or pain" (v. 4).

The tears of a friend helped a Michigan player get into his only game and earn a letter.

Dan Cline was a three-year UM letterman in both football and baseball. He was a starting safety and halfback from 1952-54. As a senior, he led the Big Ten in kickoff returns and the team in rushing yards, passing yards, and all-purpose yards. He was the baseball team captain his senior year ('55). In 1954 he led the team in hitting and the Big Ten in slugging. His sophomore year he hit .500 in the 1953 College World Series for the national champions. He was inducted into the Michigan Hall of Honor in 2007.

On Nov. 13, 1954, Cline played against Michigan State in his last home football game as a Wolverine. He threw a pass to starting quarterback Lou Baldacci that went for 67 yards and a touchdown that blew the game open at 33-7. With Ohio State still to play and this game well in hand, head coach Bennie Oosterbaan pulled him out.

Cline trotted to the bench and sat down next to his friend and roommate Jim Bowman, a third-string senior center who had never played a game. As he sat there, Cline suddenly broke into tears. He was crying because the realization had hit him that this was his last home game. There was more to it, though, than that.

Oosterbaan looked over, saw the tears, and approached him. "What is the matter?" he asked his star. Cline answered him with a request. "Put Bowman in," he begged.

The head coach looked at Cline for a moment and then he pointed toward the field and shouted, "Get in there, Bowman."

Bowman put on his helmet and trotted onto the field for the first and last time in his Michigan career. He played the rest of the game and earned a letter.

When your parents died. When a friend revealed to you she was divorcing. When you broke your collarbone as a child. When you watch a sad movie.

You cry. Crying is as much a part of life as are breathing, over-priced movie popcorn, and potholes on the highway. Usually our tears are brought on by pain, sorrow, or disappointment.

But what about when your first child was born? When Michigan beats Ohio State? When you discovered Jesus Christ? Those times elicit tears too because we cry at the times of our greatest, most overwhelming joy.

Thus, while there will be tears in Heaven, they will be tears of sheer, unmitigated, undiluted joy. The greatest joy possible, a joy beyond our imagining, must occur when we finally see Christ. If we shed tears when Michigan wins a game, can we really believe that we will stand dry-eyed and calm in the presence of Jesus?

What we will not shed in Heaven are tears of sorrow and pain.

I was sitting on the bench with tears running down my face.
-- Dan Cline on the '54 Michigan State game

Tears in Heaven will be like everything else there:
a part of the joy we will experience.

DAY 88

KEEP OUT!

Read Exodus 26:31-35; 30:1-10.

"The curtain will separate the Holy Place from the Most Holy Place" (v. 26:33).

What am I doing here?" Phil Seymour repeatedly asked himself that question while he was playing football for Michigan.

The first time Seymour figured that maybe he didn't belong was in the fall of 1967 when he made the traveling squad for the season opener as a freshman. He was not by any means a typical linebacker. He weighed only 190 pounds and was tall and slender.

Against Duke in that opener, he was on the sideline watching his mentor, middle linebacker Tom Stincic. The defense held and as they trotted off the field, Stincic separated from the group. To Seymour's shock, Stincic was covered with blood. His pants were stained, and his face and arms were dripping blood and sweat. "What am I doing here?" Seymour asked himself out loud. "My mom didn't raise a fool. I better get outta here."

Despite feeling like he didn't belong, Seymour hung around a while and got his first start that season against Minnesota. Early in the game, Tom Goss, who was playing next to Seymour, dislocated an elbow. (See Devotion No. 80.) After Goss left the field, the defense huddled up again. Linebacker Rocky Rosema stumbled into the huddle, looked at Seymour, and asked, "Where am I?"

Seymour pondered his situation for a moment. He weighed all of 190 pounds, he had just seen one of his guys carted off the field

WOLVERINES

with a somewhat gruesome injury, and another one of his guys was "talking goofy." To top that off, a Gopher player suddenly said, "We got two of them on that play; let's get some more."

Right about then, Seymour asked himself once again what in the world he was doing playing football.

Gradually, though, Seymour came to feel like an insider, and that persistent voice of doubt in his head grew quiet. He won All-Big Ten honors twice and was a first-team Academic All-America.

That civic club with its elite membership by invitation only. The bleachers where you sit while others frolic in the sky boxes. That neighborhood you can't afford a house in. You know all about being shut out of some club, some group, some place. "Exclusive" is the word that keeps you out.

The Hebrew people, too, knew about being told to keep out; only the priests could come into the presence of the holy and survive. Then along came Jesus to kick that barrier down and give us direct access to God.

In the process, though, Jesus created another exclusive club; its members are his followers, Christians, those who believe he is the Son of God and the savior of the world. This club, though, extends a membership invitation to everyone in the whole wide world; no one is excluded. Whether you're in or out depends on your response to Jesus, not on arbitrary gatekeepers.

There are clubs you can't belong to, neighborhoods you can't live in, schools you can't get into, but the roads are always open.

-- *Nike*

Christianity is an exclusive club, but an invitation is extended to everyone and no one is denied entry.

DAY 89

A ROARING SUCCESS

Read Galatians 5:16-26.

"So I say, live by the Spirit. . . . The sinful nature desires what is contrary to the Spirit. . . . I warn you, as I did before, that those who live like this will not inherit the kingdom of God" (vv. 16, 17, 21).

He was born in an internment camp and stood only 5′5″ full grown -- not exactly a formula for hockey success. And yet he was one of Michigan's greatest players.

Mel Wakabayashi has been called "perhaps the most unlikely star in the long history of Michigan sports, and surely one of the most inspirational." With World War II raging in 1942, the Canadian government relocated Wakabayashi's Japanese-born parents from their Vancouver home to a barren camp. A year later, Mel was born. The family was imprisoned until the war was over, living in frigid cold and in unsanitary stables and barnyards.

The family then moved to a small town in Ontario. "It was a good life," Wakabayashi said. Here he and his younger brother began to play pond hockey and street hockey, and gradually Mel's reputation spread. "Of course I dreamed of playing in the NHL one day," Wakabayashi said, "but knowing my size, I didn't think it would ever be a reality."

But other boys from the town had attended Michigan to play hockey, and apparently one of them alerted UM head coach Al Renfrew. He scouted Wakabayashi and that was that. In the fall of 1963, the 5'5" hockey player born in a camp came to Ann Arbor.

He became a legend. He scored two goals in the championship game as the Wolverines won the 1964 national title. He was All-America in '65 and both the league's leading scorer and its Player of the Year in 1966. He went on to play in the Japan Ice Hockey League, and in 2006 he achieved the ultimate in sports success for a Michigan athlete: He was inducted into the university's athletic hall of fame.

Are you a successful person? Your answer, of course, depends upon how you define success. Is the measure of your success based on the number of digits in your bank balance, the square footage of your house, or that title on your office door?

Certainly the world determines success by wealth, fame, prestige, awards, and possessions. Our culture screams that life is all about gratifying your own needs and wants. If it feels good, do it. It's basically the Beach Boys' philosophy of life.

But all success of this type has one glaring shortcoming: You can't take it with you. Eventually, Daddy takes the T-bird away. Like life itself, all these things are fleeting.

A more lasting and meaningful way to approach success is through the spiritual rather than the physical. The goal becomes not money or backslaps by sycophants but eternal life spent with God. Success of that kind is forever.

If you coach for 25 years and never win a championship but you influence three people for Christ, that is success.
-- Oklahoma women's basketball coach Sherri Coale

Success isn't permanent, and failure isn't fatal -- unless it's in your relationship with God.

DAY 90

TIME FOR A CHANGE

Read Romans 6:1-14.

"Just as Christ was raised from the dead through the glory of the Father, we too may live a new life" (v. 4).

Michigan once beat Southern Cal so badly in the Rose Bowl that the Associated Press changed the way it decided its national champion -- at least temporarily.

Time magazine said they ran "a baffling assortment of double-reverses, laterals, criss-crosses, quick hits, and spins." One sportswriter said the backfield was "full of pervasive shadows that fit about like wraiths." They were the "Mad Magicians" of 1947.

While many other college teams were switching to the T formation, Michigan head coach Fritz Crisler was putting an offense on the field that used the old single wing in a way no one had ever seen before. That is, no one had ever seen "a team on which the ball was liable to end up in anyone's hands at any time."

The basis of Crisler's offensive philosophy was deception. The Mad Magicians practiced it to such an extent that even Crisler often lost track of the ball from the sideline.

Every play went through Michigan's great spinning fullback, Jack Weisenburger. Once he got the ball, the play could be "a reverse, a buck lateral, a spin to the halfback or circling end, or a quick hitter." If that weren't confusing enough, every play could be run out of seven different formations.

Despite his use of the single wing, Crisler was not a hidebound traditionalist. Through his creative handling of substitutes, he is generally credited with giving birth to two-platoon football.

The Mad Magicians lost only to Notre Dame and finished No. 8 in the final Associated Press poll. But when they went out to Pasadena and waxed Southern California 49-0 in the Rose Bowl, the AP decided a change was necessary. The pollsters voted again and named the Wolverines the nation's top team.

Only after Notre Dame partisans raised a ruckus did the AP change its mind again and name the Irish its "official" champ.

Anyone who asserts no change is needed in his or her life just isn't paying attention. Every life has doubt, worry, fear, failure, frustration, unfulfilled dreams, and unsuccessful relationships in some combination. The memory and consequences of our past often haunt and trouble us.

Simply recognizing the need for change in our lives, though, doesn't mean the changes that will bring about hope, joy, peace, and fulfillment will occur. We need some power greater than ourselves or we wouldn't be where we are.

So where can we turn to? Where lies the hope for a changed life? It lies in an encounter with the Lord of all Hope: Jesus Christ. For a life turned over to Jesus, change is inevitable. With Jesus in charge, the old self with its painful and destructive ways of thinking, feeling, loving, and living is transformed.

A changed life is always only a talk with Jesus away.

Change is an essential element of sports, as it is of life.
-- *Erik Brady*, USA Today

**In Jesus lie the hope and the power
that change lives.**

DAY 91

IN A WORD

Read Matthew 12:33-37.

"For out of the overflow of the heart the mouth speaks. The good man brings good things out of the good stored up in him, and the evil man brings evil things out of the evil stored up in him" (vv. 34b-35).

Tom Ziemann could think of only one thing to say to comfort his son: "Hey, you've been through this once before."

As a sophomore, Chris Ziemann was the starting right guard for the 1997 national champions. In 1998, though, his season ended early with an injury in the Big Ten opener against Michigan State.

As he had done so many times before, Ziemann pulled to his right on a running play and locked on a linebacker. A defender dove for the running back and missed. Instead, he rolled onto Ziemann's right ankle. "I never saw it coming," he said.

Medics put an air cast on his right leg and got him to the sideline. "I was sitting there, and the doctors took off my shoe," Ziemann recalled. "My leg flopped the wrong way, and that's when I kind of figured I'd be out for a while."

Chris' dad was there when his son came out of surgery on Monday. He tried to encourage his son with a few jokes, "but jokes don't work on players who are out for the rest of the season." So he said the only thing he could come up with that seemed appropriate: "You've been through this once before."

Chris had. After leaving the first contact football practice of

WOLVERINES

his junior season, he lost control of his car when he hit some railroad tracks. He drove into the side of a post office. As dad put it, "That was the end of the season."

But Ziemann fought his way back for the second half of the basketball season and for his senior year of football. That's what his father was referring to.

Just as he had done before, Chris Ziemann salvaged his senior season. He started for the Wolverines for all of 1999.

These days, everybody's got something to say and likely as not a place to say it. Talk radio, 24-hour sports and news TV channels, late-night talk shows. Talk has really become cheap.

But words -- such as those of a father comforting a son -- still have power, and that includes not just those of the talking heads, hucksters, and pundits on television, but ours also. Our words are perhaps the most powerful force we possess for good or for bad. The words we speak today can belittle, wound, humiliate, and destroy. They can also inspire, heal, protect, and create. Our words both shape and define us. They also reveal to the world the depth of our faith.

We should never make the mistake of underestimating the power of the spoken word. After all, speaking the Word was the only means Jesus had to get his message across – and look what he managed to do.

We must always watch what we say, because others sure will.

Don't talk too much or too soon.

-- *Bear Bryant*

Choose your words carefully; they are the most powerful force you have for good or for bad.

PRAYER WARRIORS

Read Luke 18:1-8.

"Then Jesus told his disciples a parable to show them that they should always pray and not give up" (v. 1).

P lease, God, let me do something to make a difference." Billy Taylor's prayer was answered in a big way.

Taylor was an All-American running back who from 1969-71 broke the Michigan career rushing record with 3,072 yards. The Wolverines entered the '71 Ohio State game unbeaten, having already clinched the Big Ten title. The team MVP that year, Taylor was the leading rusher for the third straight season.

As the Wolverines had done to the Buckeyes two years before in the mammoth 24-12 upset of '69, Ohio State seemed determined to end Michigan's undefeated season. The Bucks used a long punt return and a stout defense to lead 7-3 when Michigan got the ball back for what would probably be its last chance.

With backup quarterback Larry Cipa leading the run-oriented offense, the Wolverines calmly moved down the field. "Slowly but surely, Michigan moved toward the winning score, and Taylor was waiting to plunge a dagger into the Buckeyes' hearts."

With less than three minutes to play, Michigan sat at the Ohio State 21 "It was do or die," Taylor remembered. The situation was so tense that he figured a little divine help wouldn't hurt, so he prayed, asking God to let him make a difference.

Head coach Bo Schembechler changed the play that had been

called to get the ball to his workhorse. Cipa pitched to Taylor, who got a block from wide receiver Bo Rather and then followed full-back Fritz Seyferth around the corner.

"My feet weren't even touching the ground," Taylor said. After Seyferth's block, he beat the only Buckeye who had a shot at him and scored for the 10-7 Michigan win. "I couldn't even breathe," he said. "I never will forget that moment."

That's the usual reaction when God answers a prayer.

Billy Taylor prayed and sprung into action, which is what Jesus taught us to do as his followers: always pray and never give up.

Any problems we may have with prayer and its results derive from our side, not God's. We pray for a while about something – perhaps fervently at first – but our enthusiasm wanes if we don't receive the answer we want exactly when we want it. Why waste our time by asking for the same thing over and over again?

But God isn't deaf; God does hear our prayers, and God does respond to them. As Jesus clearly taught, our prayers have an impact because they turn the power of Almighty God loose in this world. Thus, falling to our knees and praying to God is not a sign of weakness and helplessness. Rather, praying for someone or something is an aggressive act, an intentional ministry, a conscious and fervent attempt on our part to change someone's life or the world for the better.

God responds to our prayers; we often just can't perceive or don't understand how he is making those prayers come about.

I remember raising my hands to the sky after I scored to thank God.
-- Billy Taylor on the play that answered his prayer

Jesus taught us to always pray and never give up.

DAY 93

CHANCE MEETING

Read Luke 24:13-35.

"That same day two of them were going to a village. . . .
They were talking with each other about everything that
had happened. . . . Jesus himself came up and walked
along with them" (vv. 13-15).

Just like in the movies, boy on a date literally bumps into a girl he's just seen around. That chance meeting not only changed their lives but the history of Michigan volleyball as well.

Mark Rosen was playing collegiate volleyball when he went to a high school tournament to watch a highly touted sophomore. They didn't even talk to each other that night.

Over the years, their paths crossed because of the common interest in volleyball, but the game was their only link. He was eight years older, and their lives were going different ways.

Until the fall of 1991 when she was playing in the Final Four for Ohio State and he was there as an assistant coach for the University of Alaska. As Rosen and his date left the venue one night, he turned a corner and physically bumped into her. For the first time, he thought, "I might ask this girl out."

They were both from Alaska where "the volleyball circle . . . is as big as the ice-fishing circle in Hawaii." He did indeed ask her out over Christmas -- for a game of volleyball. "Neither of us really knew if it was a date or just volleyball," Rosen said. Whatever it was, it worked.

WOLVERINES

Mark Rosen and Leisa Wissler were married in May 1993. In one of the more unusual arrangements in college athletics, they came to Ann Arbor as a team in 1999 to coach volleyball.

With Mark as the head coach and Leisa as the associate head coach, they constitute the most successful coaching staff in UM volleyball history. Through the 2011 season, the Rosens had won 261 matches, the most of any coach, and had led the team into six consecutive NCAA tournaments and nine of the last ten.

It all started when they accidentally bumped into each other.

Maybe you met your spouse on a blind date, at a Michigan football game, or in Meijer's frozen food section. Perhaps a conversation in an elevator or over lunch led to a job offer.

Chance meetings often shape our lives. Some meetings, however, are too important to be left to what seem like the whims of life. If your child is sick, you don't wait until you happen to bump into a physician at Starbucks to seek help.

So it is with Jesus. Too much is at stake to leave a meeting with him to chance. Instead, you intentionally seek him at church, in the pages of your Bible, on your knees in prayer, or through a conversation with a friend or neighbor. How you conduct the search doesn't matter; what matters is that you find him.

Once you've met him, you should then intentionally cultivate the acquaintance until it is a deep, abiding, life-shaping and life-changing friendship.

We come around a corner, and she's with her mom and her club coach.
-- Mark Rosen on his chance meeting with Leisa Wissler

A meeting with Jesus should not be a chance encounter, but instead should be sought out.

DAY 94

LIVE ACTION

Read James 2:14-26.

"Faith by itself, if it is not accompanied by action, is dead"
(v. 17).

Just a routine press conference -- that's all it was. Until Michigan quarterback Jim Harbaugh started talking.

Quite simply, Harbaugh is one of the greatest quarterbacks in Wolverine football history. A three-year starter (1984-86), he was the Big Ten Player of the Year as a senior and finished third in the voting for the Heisman Trophy. He was twice All-America and led the nation in passing efficiency in 1985, setting a record that stood for twelve years.

At a press conference the Monday before the Ohio State game of 1986, Harbaugh suddenly guaranteed that the Wolverines would beat the Buckeyes and land the berth in the Rose Bowl. "We're going to be jacked up and we're going to win," he said.

As usual, the game didn't really need any more attention. UM was ranked No. 6, OSU No. 7, with the Big-Ten title and the Rose-Bowl berth on the line. But Harbaugh's words made sure the spotlight shined even brighter on the game -- and on him.

Head coach Bo Schembechler shrugged off his quarterback's words. "He's 22 years old, so he can say whatever he wants," he said. His counterpart in Columbus likewise didn't get too excited about the talk. "The game is played on the football field," the head Buckeye said. "It is not won by talking." Still, the OSU practice facility that week was festooned with pictures of Harbaugh, and each one had "guarantee" scrawled across it.

OSU led 14-6 at halftime, but Harbaugh delivered in the second half. He led two TD drives and then hit Bob Perryman for a score on a 23-yard screen pass. The lead was 26-17.

In the end, the senior quarterback had done all he could to guarantee his guarantee. He completed 19 passes for 261 yards and a touchdown. And in the end, the game came down to a field goal try that went wide left. Michigan won 26-24.

Asked about Harbaugh's guarantee after the game, Schembechler replied, "I'd have said it myself if I had any guts."

Talk is cheap. Consider your neighbor or coworker who talks without saying anything, who makes promises she doesn't keep, who brags about his own exploits, who can always tell you how to do something but never shows up for the work.

How often have you fidgeted through a meeting, impatient to get on with the work everybody is talking about doing? You know – just as Jim Harbaugh knew against Ohio State in 1986 -- that speech without action just doesn't cut it.

That principle applies in the life of a person of faith too. Merely declaring our faith isn't enough, however sincere we may be. It is putting our faith into action that shouts to the world of the depth of our commitment to Christ. Just as Jesus' ministry was a virtual whirlwind of activity, so are we to change the world by doing.

Jesus Christ is alive; so should our faith in Him be.

I knew if I made that kind of statement, I would have to back it up.
-- Jim Harbaugh on the '86 OSU game

Faith that does not reveal itself in action is dead.

DAY 95

ANSWERING THE CALL

Read 1 Samuel 3:1-18.

"The Lord came and stood there, calling as at the other times, 'Samuel! Samuel!' Then Samuel said, 'Speak, for your servant is listening'" (v. 10).

David Baas answered the call when his team needed him. He wound up playing three different positions -- and being named the best in the country at the third one.

Baas started high school in Florida as a trumpet player in the band. Everything changed one day when the football coach saw this big kid blowing a horn. "No, no," he said. "You come with me." David Baas the football player was born.

Baas' arrival in Ann Arbor in 2000 was rather ignominious. He had hurt a knee late in his senior season and had then tweaked it in an all-star game. The medical staff told him he needed surgery and advised him to go ahead with it since he would be redshirted anyhow. That meant Baas spent a year without knowing his teammates very well. "Some of them called me 'the Ghost,'" he said because they had no idea whether he was any good or not.

But he was.

Baas came to Ann Arbor as a tackle, but he stayed there "for possibly a week," he said. The team needed guards, so for the first time he answered the call and moved to a new position.

He got his first start in 2002 as a redshirt sophomore. His primary recollection of the game is of missing a block and turning around to yell at quarterback John Navarre to duck. It didn't help; Navarre got sacked.

Before long, though, Baas wasn't getting beaten as he made some thirty straight starts at guard. But in his senior season of 2004, the call came again. The week before the fourth game of the season, against Iowa, the coaches asked Baas to move to center. He answered the call again and played so well that he became the first center in Michigan history to win the Rimington Trophy as the nation's best center.

A team player is someone like David Baas who does whatever the coach calls upon him to do for the good of the team. Something quite similar occurs when God places a specific call upon a Christian's life.

This is much scarier, though, than shifting positions on a football team as David Baas did. The way many folks understand it is that answering God's call means going into the ministry, packing the family up, and moving halfway around the world to some place where folks have never heard of central heating, ice hockey, paved roads, or the Wolverines. Zambia. The Philippines. New York even.

Not for you, no thank you. And who can blame you?

But God usually calls folks to serve him where they are. In fact, God put you where you are right now, and he has a purpose in placing you there. Wherever you are, you are called to serve him.

You have to go in there. We have plenty of confidence in you.
      — The coaches' call to David Baas to play center

God calls you to serve him right now
right where he has put you, wherever that is.

DAY 96

PRACTICE SESSION

Read 2 Peter 1:3-11.

"For if you do these things, you will never fail, and you will receive a rich welcome into the eternal kingdom of our Lord and Savior Jesus Christ" (vv. 10b-11).

Bo Schembechler knew one thing for sure about his team when he arrived in Ann Arbor in 1969: They were soft. Practice would change that.

From the first day, Schembechler ran "ferocious practices, the likes of which none of [the players] had ever experienced." "We got after it in practice," said tackle Jim Brandstatter. Schembechler carried a yardstick at those practices and swatted players with it when they made a mistake. He declared that "a Michigan team might lose but it would never be outhit." As a result, "the walk-ons quit in droves." Schembechler's response was to put up a sign that promised, "Those who stay will be champions."

The physical practices didn't necessarily exclude the coach. During a scrimmage, he was on the sideline calling the plays and sending them in. As a play was being run, he was already looking over his notes to call the next play. One play, though, came his way, and he didn't look up until it was too late to get out of the way. Several players plowed into him full-speed.

As Brandstatter put it, "Bo was upended, his hat flew one way, the papers another, and his body yet another." Linebacker Mike Taylor was among the crowd that ambushed Schembechler. He recalled that it got very quiet. The coach struggled to his feet and barked, "Where's my hat?"

When it was retrieved, he put it back on and wobbled to the sideline, the field still strangely quiet. He looked around at everyone and then dropped his gaze to his play sheet. Without looking up, he said, "That would have killed any ordinary human!"

The practices were tough, but so was their head coach.

Imagine a football team that never practices or a play cast that doesn't rehearse. Consider also a preacher who never prepares or reviews his sermons beforehand. When the moment comes, they would be revealed as inept bumblers that merit our disdain.

We practice something so that we will become good at it, so that it becomes so natural that we can pull it off without even having to think about it. Interestingly, if we are to live as Christ wants us to, then we must practice that lifestyle – and showing up at church and sitting stoically on a pew once a week does not constitute practice. To practice successfully, we must participate; we must do repeatedly whatever it is we want to be good at.

We must practice being like Christ by living like Christ every day of our lives. For Christians, practice is a lifestyle that doesn't make perfect -- only Christ is perfect – but it does prepare us for the real thing: the day we meet God face to face and inherit Christ's kingdom.

Our practices were not for the faint of heart.
-- Tackle Jim Brandstatter in 1969

Practicing the Christian lifestyle doesn't make us perfect, but it does secure us a permanent place beside the perfect one.

DAY 97

BLIND JUSTICE

Read Micah 6:6-8.

"He has showed you, O man, what is good. And what does the Lord require of you? To act justly and to love mercy and to walk humbly with your God" (v. 8).

What the NCAA did to Michigan's hockey team in 1990 was unjust. Yet it may have been the last step in the creation of the powerhouse that the sport is today.

In the late 1980s, the Wolverine hockey program was so bad that its survival was in doubt. Three years into his tenure as head coach, after the 1986-87 season, Red Berenson's record was a dismal 39-77-2.

But the situation was worse than wins and losses: The program was hemorrhaging money. The average crowd for a game was about 500. Athletic director Don Canham had gotten to the point where he wondered if the program was worth either the trouble or the expense.

Berenson knew what he was doing, and the woeful program improved. The team went 24-12-6 in 1989-90, ending the season by whipping Bowling Green in the consolation game of the Central Collegiate Hockey Association's tournament.

The Wolverines thus sat on the NCAA tournament bubble and their first trip since 1977. One night later, Berenson got the call. The selection committee had gone with Bowling Green.

Reaction in Ann Arbor was visceral. UM hockey historian John

U. Bacon called the selection "an inside job" because Bowling Green's athletic director was on the four-man committee. "He clearly homered them. . . . It was grossly unfair."

Even so, Bacon always felt that the injustice helped turn the program around. "Out of the pain of that experience, the seeds for their 20 years of success were sown," Bacon said.

As of the 2011-12 season, that was 22 NCAA tournaments ago. The Wolverines were in every one of them.

Where's the justice when cars fly past you just as a state trooper pulls you over? When a con man swindles an elderly neighbor? When crooked politicians treat your tax dollars as their personal slush fund? When children starve?

Injustice enrages us, but anger by itself is not enough. The establishment of justice in this world has to start with each one of us. The Lord requires it of us. For most of us, a just world is one in which everybody gets what he or she deserves.

But that is not God's way. God expects us to be just and merciful in all our dealings without consideration as to whether the other person "deserves" it. The justice we dispense should truly be blind.

If that doesn't sound "fair," then pause and consider that when we stand before God, the last thing we want is what we deserve. We want mercy, not justice.

I felt devastated. I just think we were shafted.
-- Red Berenson on not making the '90 tournament

God requires that we dispense justice and mercy
without regards to deserts, exactly what we pray
we will in turn receive from God.

CLOTHES HORSE

Read Genesis 37:1-11.

*"Israel loved Joseph more than all his children, because
he was the son of his old age: and he made him a coat of
many colours" (v. 3 KJV).*

Fritz Crisler certainly had aesthetics in mind when he designed
the most iconic helmet in college football, but he was also seeking
a competitive advantage.

As many other teams did, Michigan wore basic black football
helmets when Crisler arrived in Ann Arbor in 1938 to begin a new
era in football. Before he was through after the 1947 season, Crisler "took Michigan into the modern era and initiated the second
great dynasty in the school's football history." One of the ways
Crisler moved the Wolverines into the modern era was by ditch-
ing those old black helmets.

At the time, some teams tended to use different colored helmets
for receivers, but Crisler discarded that notion. "I always thought
that would be as helpful for the defense as for the offense," he
explained. Crisler had tinkered with the iconic winged design of
the helmet at Princeton, introducing a helmet remarkably similar
to Michigan's. His major innovation in Ann Arbor was to paint
the helmet maize and blue.

In introducing the unique helmets, Crisler was at heart seeking
an advantage on the field. His offense was based on a quick-strike
aerial attack that depended on his passer being able to spot his

receivers downfield as soon as possible. The distinctive winged helmet gave the quarterback an immediate visual clue.

The helmet debuted in the 1938 season opener, a 14-0 win over Michigan State. Newspaper accounts of the game didn't mention the innovative hats. Whether the helmet helped or not, the 1938 team nearly doubled its passing yardage versus 1937 and cut interceptions in half.

Contemporary society proclaims that it's all about the clothes, even a spiffy helmet for the football team. Buy that new suit or dress, those new shoes, and all the accessories, and you'll be a new person.

The changes are only cosmetic, though; under all those clothes, you're the same person. Consider Joseph, for instance, prancing about in his pretty new clothes; he was still a spoiled little tattletale whom his brothers detested enough to sell into slavery.

Jesus never taught that we should run around half-naked or wear only second-hand clothes from the local mission. He did warn us, though, against making consumer items such as clothes a priority in our lives. A follower of Christ seeks to emulate Jesus not through material, superficial means such as wearing special clothing like a robe and sandals. Rather, the disciple desires to match Jesus' inner beauty and serenity -- whether the clothes the Christian wears are the sables of a king or the rags of a pauper.

Through all the changes [in helmet design], Michigan has preserved the design [Fritz] Crisler imported to add a bit of style to Michigan's look.
-- Anonymous article on Michigan's winged helmet

**Where Jesus is concerned,
clothes don't make the person; faith does.**

DAY 99

WHAT YOU HAVE TO

Read 2 Samuel 12:1-15a.

"The Lord sent Nathan to David" (v. 1).

Football players routinely do what they have to in order to help their team win a football game. Nobody in Michigan gridiron history, however, has ever carried that basic premise to the extreme that Vincent Smith did against Minnesota in 2011.

At his news conference on Monday, Sept. 19, head coach Brady Hoke announced that Smith, a junior, had "earned the right" to be the team's lead running back. That made him the third starting tailback in four games for the undefeated Wolverines, following sophomore Fitz Toussaint and senior Michael Shaw.

Hoke admitted he and offensive coordinator Al Borges didn't like the notion of tailback-by-committee, but they had so much talent on hand they liked the versatility they had at that position.

They couldn't imagine, though, the versatility that Smith alone brought to the offense against Minnesota on Oct. 1 in his second start. Smith put on a one-man variety show, accomplishing something that had never before been done by a UM football player.

On the first drive of the game, quarterback Denard Robinson simply handed the ball off to Smith, who scored on a 3-yard run for the first of Michigan's many touchdowns on the day. On the Wolverines' third possession, Robinson again handed the ball to Smith, only this time he suddenly stopped short and lofted a pass to sophomore wide receiver Drew Dileo for a score.

WOLVERINES

But Smith wasn't through. Midway through the second period, he caught a short pass from Robinson and turned it into a 28-yard touchdown play.

Smith thus did something that had never before been done by a Wolverine, at least not since football became the game we know today. In a single game, he scored touchdowns via running, passing, and receiving.

Smith just did what he had to for his team. Michigan won 58-0.

You've done some thing in your life simply because you had to that weren't as pleasant as Vincent Smith's touchdown trifecta. Maybe when you put your daughter on severe restriction, broke the news of a death in the family, fired a friend, or underwent surgery. You plowed ahead because you knew it was for the best or you had no choice.

Nathan surely didn't want to confront King David and tell him what a miserable reprobate he'd been, but the prophet didn't have a choice: Obedience to God overrode all other factors. Of all that God asks of us in the living of a godly life, obedience is perhaps the most difficult. After all, our history of disobedience stretches all the way back to the Garden of Eden.

The problem is that God expects obedience not only when his wishes match our own but also when they don't. Obedience to God is a way of life, not a matter of convenience.

[I'll do] whatever I have to do for the team to help them out.
-- Vincent Smith after the 2011 Minnesota game

You can never foresee what God
will demand of you, but obedience requires
being ready to do whatever God asks.

DAY 100

THE END

Read Revelation 22:1-17.

*"I am the Alpha and the Omega, the First and the Last,
the Beginning and the End" (v. 13).*

At the end of his Michigan football career, Rick Leach cried along with the man most responsible for its beginning.

Leach was a star quarterback for the Wolverines from 1975-78, an All-America in both football and baseball. A starter as a freshman, he shattered all of Michigan's career passing, total offense, and touchdown records.

Out of high school, Leach had the problem of not only deciding which college to attend but which sport to play -- especially when the Philadelphia Phillies threw a six-figure offer his way. Leach recalled, "My first reaction was, 'Where's the pen? Let's get this done!'" But his father said to the Phillies scout, "Can you give us some time? I want to talk to my son."

Leach's dad was a Michigan man who had played on the 1953 national champion baseball team. He told Rick if the money were most important to him, it would still be available if he went to Michigan. Leach Senior then went on to speak glowingly about the Michigan experience. "I just had the kind of relationship and love for my dad that, thank God, I had at least composure enough to listen and believe in what he told me," Rick said.

That love and relationship revealed itself four years later on Nov. 25, 1978, after Leach quarterbacked the Wolverines to a 14-3 win over Ohio State. The 10-1 team was headed to the Rose Bowl, but Leach felt this was really his last game.

He could barely walk from a hamstring injury he suffered in the game, so he was sitting at his locker jubilant but hurting and out of energy when he saw his dad. "I don't know how he got in," he said. His father didn't say a word. "He sat down, hugged me, and we both just started crying," Leach said.

College football was basically over for Rick Leach, but the relationship with his dad was not. "That's one of the special moments I'll have till I go," Leach said.

Like Rick Leach's time at Michigan, everything ends. Even the stars have a life cycle, though admittedly it's rather lengthy. Erosion eventually will wear a boulder down to a pebble. Life itself is temporary; all living things have a beginning and an end.

Within the framework of our individual lifetimes, we experience endings. Loved ones, friends, and pets die; relationships fracture; jobs dry up; our health, clothes, lawn mowers, TV sets – they all wear out. Even this world as we know it will end.

But one of the great ironies of God's gift of life is that not even death is immune from the great truth of creation that all things must end. That's because through Jesus' life, death, and resurrection, God himself acted to end any power death once had over life. In other words, because of Jesus, the end of life has ended. Eternity is ours for the claiming.

It was the culmination of the end.
-- Rick Leach on the moments with his dad after the '78 OSU game

**Everything ends; thanks to Jesus Christ,
so does death.**

NOTES
(by Devotion Day Number)

1   In the fall of 1878, a letter . . . Purple Stockings from Racine College. "1879 Michigan Wolverines Football Team," *Wikipedia, the free encyclopedia*, http://en.wikipedia.org/wiki/1879_Michigan_Wolverines_football_team.

1   Twelve players represented Michigan, taking the train to Chicago: George Cantor, *Michigan Football: Yesterday & Today* (Lincolnwood, IL: West Side Publishing, 2008), p. 10.

1   and a bus to the playing . . . David DeTarr kicked the goal.: "1879 Michigan Wolverines Football Team."

1   One very important point must . . . we win the first game.: "1879 Michigan Wolverines Football Team."

2   "When it's 0:00 on the clock, that's the only time the game is over,": Mike Lopresti, "Michigan Leaves Notre Dame Feeling Blue," *USATODAY.com*, Sept. 12, 2011, http://www.usatoday.com/sports/columnist/lopresti/story/2011-09-11.

2   "Coach took a stab,": "Michigan Scores with 2 Seconds Left, Stuns Irish," *ESPN.com*, Sept. 10, 2011, http://scores.espn.go.com/ncf/recap?gameId=312530130.

2   It was a heart-pounding, . . . lights at the Big House: "Michigan Scores with 2 Seconds Left."

3   without ever seeing the campus . . . This kid was really good.: Joanne C. Gerstner, "The Accidental All-American," *M Magazine*, Winter 2010, p. 26, http://viewer.zmags.com/publication/a016c4aa#/a016c411/26.

3   I have to say I was . . . your office off the street.: Gerstner, "The Accidental All-American," p. 26.

4   In the 1975 game against Baylor, . . . which the Bears were driving.: Jim Brandstatter, *Tales from Michigan Stadium* (Champaign, IL: Sports Publishing L.L.C., 2002), p. 36.

4   A frantic Falk raced to . . . to get that pylon set.": Brandstatter, *Tales from Michigan Stadium*, p. 36.

4   I wasn't trying to cheat anybody. I just couldn't make it fast enough.: Brandstatter, *Tales from Michigan Stadium*, p. 37.

5   What Oosterbaan saw prior . . . great football player.": Brandstatter, *Tales from Michigan Stadium Volume II* (Champaign, IL: Sports Publishing L.L.C., 2005), p. 168.

5   But what Oosterbaan also . . . the switch to Krisler,: Brandstatter, *Tales from Michigan Stadium Volume II*, p. 168.

6   he had "a fiery disposition" and that he was "prone to sideline outbursts.": "Bo Schembechler," *Wikipedia, the free encyclopedia*, http://en.wikipedia.org/wiki/Bo_Schembechler.

6   frequently wound up yelling and kicking chairs at each other.: Greg Emmanuel, *The 100-Yard War* (Hoboken, NJ: John Wiley & Sons, Inc., 2004), p. 82.

6   Schembechler often related that . . . when their tempers cooled down.: "Bo Schembechler."

6   "legendary volcanic personality," . . . walked close to the bench.": Brandstatter, *Tales from Michigan Stadium*, p. 60.

6   Against Wisconsin one year, . . . "You walk like a girl.": Brandstatter, *Tales from Michigan Stadium*, p. 60.

6   It was the biggest putdown . . . from [Bo Schembechler] to an official.: Brandstatter, *Tales from Michigan Stadium*, p. 60.

7   The analysis of the expectations for and the shortcoming sof the 1997 team is taken from George Cantor's book *Back on Top* (Dallas: Taylor Publishing Company, 1998), pp. 18-21.

7   "didn't look much like a Michigan defense from the vintage years.": Cantor, *Back on Top*, p. 21.

7   Another four-loss season did not seem out of the question.: Cantor, *Back on Top*, p. 23.

8   a walk-on goalie who had never started a game.: John U. Bacon, "Michigan Hockey's Cinderella," *Ann Arbor Chronicle*, April 15, 2011, http://annarborchronicle.com/2011/04/15/column-michigan-hockeys-cinderella.

8   Hunwick alternated with Hogan . . . and no preparation,: Bacon, "Michigan Hockey's Cinderella."

8   "The best player on the ice . . . have a full scholarship.": Bacon, "Michigan Hockey's Cinderella."

8   I've never seen any athlete . . . nailed it, both times.: Bacon, "Michigan Hockey's Cinderella."

9   Shannon made the traveling squad . . . you are all we've got left.": Kevin Allen, Nate Brown, and Art Regner, *What It Means to Be a Wolverine* (Chicago: Triumph Books, 2005), p. 98.

9   In one prep game, they . . . around end for a touchdown.: Allen, Brown, and Regner, p. 94.

9   The huddle call was simple: . . . went banana-shape over the crossbar.: Allen, Brown, and Regner, p. 100.

9   My scoring experience at the University . . . remember the rest of my life.: Allen, Brown, and Regner, p. 100.

10   the biggest fourth-quarter comeback in school history.: "Gophers Allow 28-7 Lead to Escape," *ESPN.com*, Oct. 10, 2003, http://scores.espn.go.com/ncf/recap?gameid=23840135.

10   "I've never been in a game like this,": "Gophers Allow 28-7 Lead to Escape."

10   It just speaks to the human spirit, and these kids showed tremendous spirit.: "Gophers Allow 28-7 Lead to Escape."

11   Letters to the editor complained . . . hit one of them.: Brandstatter, *Tales from Michigan Stadium Volume II*, p. 154.

11   In September 1974, the . . . "A U-M Tradition Crumbles!": Brandstatter, *Tales from Michigan Stadium Volume II*, p. 154.

11   "There was some resentment," . . . they were together.: Brandstatter, *Tales from Michigan Stadium Volume II*, p. 154.

11   They couldn't call themselves . . . colored their skin blue.: Brandstatter, *Tales from Michigan Stadium Volume II*, p. 155.

11   The women were officially . . . them and rehearsed them.: Brandstatter, *Tales from Michigan Stadium Volume II*, p. 156.

11   "By the end of the year," . . . "there was no controversy.": Brandstatter, *Tales from Michigan Stadium Volume II*, p. 156.

11   We were breaking tradition . . . at the same time.: Brandstatter, *Tales from Michigan Stadium Volume II*, p. 156.

12   head coach John Beilein deflected any . . . have a great opportunity here,': Nick Baumgardner, "Now Is the Time," *Ann Arbor.com*, Feb. 13, 2012, http://annarbor.com/sports/um-basketball/michigan-basketball-team.

12   Not until they were back in Ann . . . had beaten the Spartans.: Ben Estes, "Wolverines Hold On to Top Penn State," *The Michigan Daily*, March 4, 2012, http://www.michigandaily.com/sports/wolverines-hold.

12   You go into it . . . what champions do on this day.: Estes, "Wolverines Hold On."

13   Anderson went the wrong way on . . . we're wasting our money on you.": Allen, Brown, and Regner, p. 287.

13   It was very intimidating. It was hard, and at times I was ready to leave.: Allen, Brown, and Regner, p. 286.

14   Mike Hart was "eerily confident": Austin Murphy, "Shock Value," *Sports Illustrated*, Sept. 25, 2006, http://sportsillustrated.cnn.com/vault/article/magazine/MAG1105534/index.htm.

14   Michigan's "seriously ornery defense": Murphy, "Shock Value."

14   The last score wound up slightly . . . that did Notre Dame's secondary.": Murphy, "Shock Value."

14   He had spent the week asking . . . I knew we'd be taking some shots.: Murphy, "Shock Value."

14   Last year they were hunting us. This year we were hunting them.: Murphy, "Shock Value."

15   When his military assignment kept . . . to Madison to see me,": Andrew Lawrence, "What a Run," *Sports Illustrated*, Aug. 22, 2008, http://sportsillustrated.cnn.com/vault/article/magazine/MAG1152245/index.htm.

15   A sportswriter for the *Chicago* . . . like a demented duck.": "Elroy Hirsch," *Wikipedia, the free encyclopedia*, http://en.wikipedia.org/wiki/Elroy_Hirsch.

15   That broken field running . . . sending him veering off-course.": Lawrence, What a Run."

15   I must've looked pretty funny.: Lawrence, "What a Run."

16   Here family received a Christmas card every year from Jim Tressel: Zak Pyzik, "Split Decisions," *The Michigan Daily News*, Feb. 15, 2010, http://www.michigandaily.com/content/carmen-reynolds.

16   Christmas photos of the family . . . her decision was made.: Pyzik, "Split Decisions."

16   "It was crazy to think . . . when he went to Carmen's games.: Pyzik, "Split Decisions."

16   [My family is] flying one of . . . with a little block 'M' on it.: Joanne C. Gerstner, "Carmen Reynolds," *MGOBLUE.COM*. 23 Nov. 2011. http://www.mgoblue.com/sports/w-baskbl/spec-rel/112311aad.html.

17   Like the plot of a bad . . . and a football hero emerged.: Emmanuel, p. 60.

17   "It was 14-0, thanks solely to Trosko's two costly mistakes.": Emmanuel, p. 58.

17   "the greatest football player the University of Michigan has ever seen": Emmanuel, 59.

17   Trosko trotted back onto the field . . . broke into wild, unrestrained applause.: Emmanuel, p. 60.

18   As Notre Dame hurried to the . . . we would be all right,": Jo-Ann Barnas "Hendricks and Family Have U-M Tales to Tell," *Detroit Free Press*, Sept. 9, 1999, p. D1.

18   As time expired, Hendricks fell . . . "Hey, I'm an emotional guy," Barnas, "Hendricks and Family."

18   At least I got some highlights on ESPN.: Barnas, "Hendricks and Family."

19   He had noticed that an . . . could blow past him easily: Brandstatter, *Tales from Michigan Stadium Volume II*, p. 63.

19   The wind also played into his . . . a little minor mistake,": Brandstatter, *Tales from Michigan Stadium Volume II*, p. 64.

19   His daring play fired everyone . . . o keep on running.": Brandstatter, *Tales from Michigan Stadium Volume II*, p. 64.

19   I really wanted to make a play.: Brandstatter, *Tales from Michigan Stadium Volume II*, p. 64.

20   He was optimistic that 2005 . . . had asked him to transfer.: Scott Bell, "Rocking the Crable," *The Michigan Daily*, Oct. 26, 2006, http://www.michigandaily.com/content/rocking-crable.

21   "Maryland Soccer, established 1946." . . . the Michigan men's soccer team: Matt Slovin, "Overtime Goal Sends 'M' Soccer to First-Ever College Cup," *The Michigan Daily*, Dec. 4, 2010, http://www.michigandaily.com/content/overtime-goal.

21   Michigan coach Steve Burns . . . elevated from club status.: Slovin, "Overtime Goal."

21   "There's an expectation every . . . to be in the College Cup,": Slovin, "Overtime Goal."

22   This game is over. We've won this game.": Brandstatter, *Tales from Michigan Stadium*, p. 183.

22   The Big Ten office sent the . . . until we beat Ohio State.": Brandstatter, *Tales from Michigan Stadium*, p. 182.

22   After practice, Falk rushed over . . . had seen in the locker room.: Brandstatter, *Tales from Michigan Stadium*, pp. 182-83.

22   both head coaches expressing their shock at the outcome.: Emmanuel, p. 147.

23   Trgovac grew up in Ohio as . . . looking for in a coach,": Allen, Brown, and Regner, p. 200.

23   He went to the Michigan-Ohio State . . . "These guys are pretty cool.": Allen, Brown, and Regner, p. 201.

23   Hayes and his coaches kept after . . . I didn't say anything,": Allen, Brown, and Regner, pp. 201-202.

23   His mother told him that wherever . . . just really afraid to say it.": Allen, Brown, and

Regner, p. 202.

23   When I have decisions to make, . . . would handle this or do that.: Allen, Brown, and Regner, p. 203.

24   "I ate, slept, and dreamt baseball,": Allen, Brown, and Regner, p. 71.

24   When Michigan's head baseball coach . . . Wistert could never pitch again.: Allen, Brown, and Regner, p. 72.

24   While he was in the Corps, . . . as had his brother, Francis and Albert,.: Allen, Brown, and Regner, p. 72.

24   Getting into a routine of studying turned out to be harder than the football.: Allen, Brown, and Regner, p. 73.

24   the oldest player in Michigan football history.: Allen, Brown, and Regner, p. 74.

24   Here comes Pappy and his kids again.: Allen, Brown, and Regner, p. 71.

25   "That dream kind of left,": Cantor, Back on Top, p. 151.

25   head coach Lloyd Carr asked . . . "How about wide receiver?": Tim Layden, "Double Threat," Sports Illustrated, Nov. 18, 1996, p. 45.

25   "had taken over the game of . . . the Heisman ballots being switched": Cantor, Back on Top, p. 146.

25   During the Ohio State game, . . . closest friend on the team.: Cantor, Back on Top, p. 152.

25   Marcus, I'm going to win every award in God's power.: Cantor, Back on Top, p. 153.

26   "A Michigan man will coach . . . at 7:30 the next morning: Dana O'Neil, "Steve Fisher Had Success," ESPN. com, Feb. 22, 2008, http://sports.espn.go.com/ncb/columns/story?columnist=oneil_dana&id=3259425.

26   "college basketball's improbable princes." . . . face and voice that Fisher presented.: O'Neil, "Steve Fisher Had Success."

27   "the greatest nightmare I've ever experienced in sports,": Tim Layden, "Prayer Answered," Sports Illustrated, Sept. 23, 1996, p. 45.

27   "heaved a tight spiral 73 yards. . . of an Ann Arbor evening.": Layden, "Prayer Answered," p. 44.

27   he decided months before the rematch he would not talk about the nightmare.: Layden, "Prayer Answered," p. 45.

27   four receivers sprinting for the end zone. "I was sick,": Layden, "Prayer Answered," p. 44.

27   "Nobody said anything about two . . . Here we go again.": Layden, "Prayer Answered," p. 46.

27   We've suffered enough because of that play.: Layden, "Prayer Answered," p. 44.

28   Elliott Mealer thought God was . . . suffered two shattered vertabrae.: Amy Whitesall, "Impossible Is Nothing," M Magazine, Fall 2010, p. 12, http://viewer.zmags.com/publication/e9add83c#/e9add83c.

28   The doctors were unanimous . . . wanted me to accept that fact.": Pete Bigelow, "From 'Never' to Walking," AnnArbor.com, Sept. 2, 2010, http://www.annarbor.com/sports/um-football/from-never-to-walking.

28   Brock's physical therapy occasionally . . . get out of that wheelchair?: Whitesall, "Impossible Is Nothing," p. 13.

28   Barwis created a plan . . . that read, "Impossible Is Nothing.": Whitesall, "Impossible Is Nothing," p. 13.

28   On Sept. 4, 2010, Brock . . . the opener against Connecticut.: Whitesall, "Impossible Is Nothing," p. 12.

28   assisted by a pair of canes . . . and walked to midfield.: Whitesall, "Impossible Is Nothing," p. 15.

28   Brock Mealer had become . . . of what is possible.: Whitesall, "Impossible Is Nothing," p. 12.

28   It's up to God and Brock to make it work, and I have faith in both.: Whitesall, "Impossible Is Nothing," p. 13.

29   "we wanted to win it right here . . . "in a single, held breath": Tom Rowland, "Michigan Snaps M.S.U. Jinx," in Hail to the Victors, Francis J. Fitzgerald, ed. (Louisville, KY: AdCraft Sports Marketing, 1995), p. 111.

29   tackle Bill yearby led a defensive stand.: Rowland, p. 111.

29   It just feels real good.: Rowland, p. 112.

30   The parents hoped their son would gravitate toward soccer: Hank Hersch, "That Great Abbott Switch," Sports Illustrated, May 25, 1987, http://sportsillustrated.cnn.com/vault/article/magazine/MAG1065994/index.htm.

30   He pitched with his glove . . . and throw to the base.: John U. Bacon, "Lucky Man," Michigan Today, April 14, 2009, http://michigantoday.umich.edu/2009/04/abbott.php.

30   known as the Abbott switch.: Hersch, "That Great Abbott Switch."

30   Michigan baseball coach Bud Middaugh . . . better than I imagined.": Bacon, "Lucky Man."

30   "I don't ever remember it being something . . . was just something I did.": Bacon, "Lucky Man."

30   I want to be remembered not . . . making the most of what God gave me.: Bacon, "Lucky Man."

31   He told quarterback John Wangler, . . . this freshman talking about?: Brandstatter, Tales from Michigan Stadium, p. 49.

31   He told Carter he would get the ball to him.: Brandstatter, Tales from Michigan Stadium, p. 49.

31   A tackler knocked him off . . . with his arms raised": Brandstatter, Tales from Michigan Stadium, pp. 49-50.

31   I just had the confidence that I could make something happen.: Brandstatter, Tales from Michigan Stadium, p. 49.

32   In high school, Van Dyne sent . . . he decided to walk on.: Allen, Brown, and Regner, p. 280.

32   Schembechler always called Van . . . Washtenaw Community College.": Allen, Brown, and Regner, p. 282.

32   When Van Dyne was lackadaisical . . . what was wrong with his life.: Allen, Brown, and Regner, p. 279.

32   You're not getting the basic tenets of being successful in life.: Allen, Brown, and Regner, p. 279.

33   "I think my goal originally . . . and just survive Michigan football.": Brian Horgea, "Clock Ticking for U-M's Pollock," MLive.com, Dec. 28, 2007, http://blog.mlive.com/wolverines.stories/2007/12/clock-ticking.

33   In high school, Pollock was . . . "You're really not making any progress.": Horgea, "Clock Ticking."

33   "the coaches decided to give . . . in front of the Big House crowd.": Matt Singer, "Pollock's TD Well-Earned," The Michigan Daily, Sept. 13, 2006, http://www.michigandaily.com/content/pollocks-td-well-earned.

33   made a fingertip reception "that would have made any wide receivers' coach proud.": Singer, "Pollock's TD

Well-Earned."

33   Pollock "gained the respect of every man in our program.": Horgea, "Clock Ticking."

33   You can look at the touchdown . . . I want to start playing more.: Singer, "Pollock's TD Well-Earned."

34   They were a mostly longhaired and scruffy bunch": Tim Rohan, "A Humble Beginning," *The Michigan Daily*, Feb. 12, 2012, http://www.michigandaily.com/sports/sportsmonday-column-humble-beginning.

34   that cold February day. . . . physically imposing or impressive.": Rohan, "A Humble Beginning."

34   I will never forget this game -- though it wasn't the outcome we wanted.: Rohan, "A Humble Beginning."

35   "It was probably, to this day, . . . my career in the NFL,": Brandstatter, *Tales from Michigan Stadium Volume II*, p. 67.

35   with about six minutes left . . . bench at the 50-yard line.: Brandstatter, *Tales from Michigan Stadium Volume II*, p. 67.

35   He had given them the chance . . . rival on their home turf.: Brandstatter, *Tales from Michigan Stadium Volume II*, p. 68.

35   "All of a sudden I realized, it was dead quiet,": Brandstatter, *Tales from Michigan Stadium Volume II*, p. 67.

35   He looked across the field . . . ever played in my life,": Brandstatter, *Tales from Michigan Stadium Volume II*, p. 68.

35   There were 87,000 people in . . . couldn't hear a word.: Brandstatter, *Tales from Michigan Stadium Volume II*, p. 67.

36   "Dave Molk is the one guy . . . there in the room with her.: Stephen J. Nesbitt, "The Strongest Muscle," *The Michigan Daily*, Oct. 26, 2011, http://www.michigandaily.com/print/62746.

36   She showed me just how precious life is.: Nesbitt, "The Strongest Muscle."

37   "steamrolled the Wolverines on their way to a national championship.": Emmanuel, p. 89.

37   "were being hailed as perhaps the . . . They were a juggernaut.": Emmanuel, p. 90.

37   He had "50-14," the score of the . . . "Ohio State is beatable,": Emmanuel, p. 91.

37   The largest crowd in college football history.: Emmanuel, p. 91.

37   From the first series, "it looked like . . . about in the crisp November air.": Emmanuel, p. 93.

37   "in one of the biggest runs in Michigan football history.": Emmanuel, p. 94.

37   "one of the greatest performances I have ever seen,": Emmanuel, p. 95.

37   jubilant fans chanted "Good-bye Woody" and "We're No. 1.": Emmanuel, p. 95.

37   The revenge factor gives Michigan every incentive to win.: Emmanuel, p. 91.

38   When Greg Ryan took over . . . Hein was his first recruit.: Brad Rudner, "Soccer's Holly Hein," *M Magazine*, Fall 2011, p. 25, http://viewer.zmags.com/publication/a016c4aa#/a016c411/24.

38   During surgery in October . . . "I told them straight out,": Rudner, "Soccer's Holly Hein," p. 24.

38   "When she got into the middle . . . she dropped that on us.": Rudner, "Soccer's Holly Hein," p. 25.

38   Six days later, she was on the . . . her return to the field.: Rudner, "Soccer's Holly Hein," p. 25.

39   Athletic director Charles Baird . . . center of the national stage.: Cantor, *Michigan Football*, p. 12.

39   To that end, he scheduled . . . when it suited his purposes: Cantor, *Michigan Football*, p. 13.

39   which nearly killed the game. . . . to play a second game.: Cantor, *Michigan Football*, p. 15.

39   Critics said college . . . of a second deck.: Brandstatter, *Tales from Michigan Stadium Volume II*, p. 173.

39   "I'm interested in fitness for all,": Jim Cnockaert, *Stadium Stories: Michigan Wolverines* (Guilford, CN: The Globe Pequot Press, 2003), p. 21.

39   He had great foresight. He had great imagination.: Brandstatter, *Tales from Michigan Stadium Volume II*, p. 173.

40   The structure was built on . . . remains under the stadium.: "Facilities: Michigan Stadium," MGoBlue.com, http://www.mgoblue.com/facilities/michigan-stadium.html.

40   not long after his players . . . a pretty good game.": Brandstatter, *Tales from Michigan Stadium*, p. 192.

40   That was my first . . . affected someone else.: Brandstatter, *Tales from Michigan Stadium*, p. 192.

41   "In other seasons, the big . . . or sitting in silence.": Cantor, *Back to the Top*, p. 71.

41   "the huge throng came to its feet and began to cheer wildly.": Cantor, *Back to the Top*, pp. 71-72.

41   "To feel that kind of energy in the . . . that he could get it down,": Cantor, *Back to the Top*, p. 72.

41   it was screaming.: Cantor, *Back to the Top*, p. 72.

41   "That's when I knew this year was going to be different.": Cantor, *Back to the Top*, p. 72.

41   We were down and they were cheering like crazy.: Cantor, *Back to the Top*, p. 72.

42   "big, fast, and . . . the game with passion.": Brandstatter, *Tales from Michigan Stadium*, pp. 2-3.

42   Prior to the '70 Rose Bowl, . . . him collapsed in laughter: Allen, Brown, and Regner, p. 131.

42   "hadn't been anywhere near the physics building in his four years at Michigan.: Brandstatter, *Tales from Michigan Stadium*, p. 3.

42   The tape played, . . . come interview for a job.: Allen, Brown, and Regner, p. 131.

42   At the hospital, doctors would not . . . ushered me right on in,": Allen, Brown, and Regner, p. 132.

42   I hung out with him, . . . and then I left.: Allen, Brown, and Regner, p. 132.

43   Sometime during the 1986-87 . . . find, including dinner napkins.: Ben Estes, "Let the Ball Talk," *The Michigan Daily*, March 28, 2012, http://www.michigandaily.com/sports/let-ball-talk.

44   Late in the second quarter, . . . out of our playbook.": Kevin Wright, "Riley Excelling at Tackle," *The Michigan Daily*, Sept. 25, 2006, http://www.michigandaily.com/content/riley-excelling-tackle.

44   As a junior, he struggled . . . didn't get any holding calls.: Wright, "Riley Excelling at Tackle."

44   I saw Rueben catch it and . . . would have done the same thing.: Wright, "Riley Excelling at Tackle."

45   Lilja "waged the war . . . couldn't believe it either,": Brandstatter, *Tales from Michigan Stadium Volume II*, p. 73.

45   I am now standing on . . . shoulder pads and T-shirt.: Brandstatter, *Tales from Michigan Stadium Volume II*, p. 73.

46   In the fall of 1896, . . . gathered on Nov. 13, 1896.: "Origins of the Marching Band," *Michigan Marching Band*, http://mmb.music.umich.edu/node/43349.

46   The unusual press box presented . . . band's pre-game show,: Brandstatter, *Tales from Michigan Stadium Volume II*, p. 18.

46   "I'll do it." . . . Oklahoma quarterback.: Brandstatter, *Tales from Michigan Stadium Volume II*, p. 19.

46   *Sports Illustrated* called me an overzealous PA announcer.: Brandstatter, *Tales from Michigan Stadium Volume II*, p. 19.

47   trailing at halftime for the first time in more than a month.: Ryan Kartje, "Michigan Runs Historic Winning Streak to 16," *The Michigan Daily*, March 24, 2008, http://www.michigandaily.com/content/michigan-runs.

47   with only thirty seconds left . . . ever been a part of,": Kartje, "Michigan Runs."

47   I realized it wasn't going to work.: Kartje, "Michigan Runs."

48   He hitchhiked to and from . . . in the south end zone.: Allen, Brown, and Regner, p. 76.

48   "I hosted myself on my recruiting trip.": Allen, Brown, and Regner, p. 76.

48   He had injured a knee . . . coming off the field.: Allen, Brown, and Regner, p. 78.

48   he reinjured it in the first . . . Ted Topor, in the game.: Allen, Brown, and Regner, p. 79.

48   The game was too crucial.: Allen, Brown, and Regner, p. 79.

49   After the 1966 football season, . . . a deal with a handshake.: John U. Bacon, "Why Bo Didn't Go," *The Ann Arbor Chronicle*, Nov. 19, 2010, http://annarborchronicle.com/2010/11/19/column-why-bo-didn't-go.

50   Earlier in the week of the game of . . . "The wall doesn't move,": Emmanuel, p. 236.

50   they did so in an orderly fashion, . . . over the wall and onto the field: Emmanuel, p. 236.

50   who had to struggle to get into . . . out there than OSU's defense,": Emmanuel, p. 237.

50   ignoring the pleas from the public address . . . you are on TV; you are not.": Emmanuel, p. 236.

50   I was worried I was going to get injured with them celebrating.: Emmanuel, p. 237.

51   Big things were expected of Michigan's 2001 field hockey team.: Amy Whitesall, "Be the Boat," *M Magazine*, Fall 2011, p. 14, http://viewer.zmags.com/publication/4ea8b96d#/4ea8b96d/14.

51   the teams arrived to find . . . forever be etched in her memory.: Whitesall, "Be the Boat," p. 15.

51   the players regarded the Wolverines . . . field in our flip-flops,": Whitesall, "Be the Boat," p. 15.

51   *"despicable, vile, unprincipled scoundrels.": John MacArthur, *Twelve Ordinary Men* (Nashville: W Publishing Group, 2002), p. 152.

51   What it came down to was that we had the best team.: Whitesall, "Be the Boat," p. 15.

52   "quite possibly the best college . . . with a Tarzan physique.": Fredric Alan Maxwell, "The Late Great 98," *Michigan Today*, Sept. 17, 2008, http://michigantoday.umich.edu/2008/09/harmon.php.

52   an inebriated Cal fan made . . . Naturally, he failed.: Maxwell, "The Late Great 98."

52   when he left the field with 38 . . . to get a piece of his jersey.: Maxwell, "The Late Great 98."

52   it was so torn up he had no sleeves left.: Brandstatter, *Tales from Michigan Stadium*, p. 94.

52   When you get that from . . . thrill for all of us.: Brandstatter, *Tales from Michigan Stadium*, p. 94.

53   "the most embarrassing incident in my life as a football player.": Allen, Brown, and Regner, p. 112.

53   Mack figured he drew interest . . . particularly good high school football player.": Allen, Brown, and Regner, p. 111.

53   Mack had terrible vision but . . . or when it hit the ground.: Allen, Brown, and Regner, p. 111.

53   At Michigan, the team bought . . . "I was absolutely crushed,": Allen, Brown, and Regner, p. 112.

53   That was the highlight, or lowlight, of my sophomore year.: Allen, Brown, and Regner, p. 112.

54   In August 2011, the sophomore . . . for a Michigan comforter.: Kyle Meinke, "Michigan Receiver Drew Dileo Is Headed Home," *Ann Arbor.com*, Dec. 25, 2011, http://www.annarbor.com/sports/um-football.

54   He was in an airport . . . going to play in the Sugar Bowl.": Meinke, "Michigan Receiver Drew Dileo Is Headed Home."

54   There's no way I'm putting my hands down there.: Meinke, "Michigan Receiver Drew Dileo Is Headed Home."

55   After Bruck arrived in Ann Arbor . . . figured she needed glasses.: Sarah VanMetre, "Bruck's Battle," *M Magazine*, Fall 2011, p. 26, http://viewer.zmags.com/publication/4ea8b96d#/4ea8b96d/26.

55   When a concerned head coach . . . into going to the doctor.: Matt Florjancic, "Fight of a Lifetime," *The Chronicle-Telegram*, Jan. 19, 2011, http://chronicle.northcoastnow.com/2011/01/19/fight-of-a-lifetime.

55   After a brief interval of . . . and play volleyball again.: VanMetre, "Bruck's Battle," p. 26.

55   She was redshirted that season . . . reliability of an insulin pump: VanMetre, "Bruck's Battle," p. 27.

55   Other diabetic athletes took their . . . wanted to play volleyball.": Florjancic, "Fight of a Lifetime."

55   I started to panic at first, . . . reins of and get control of.: VanMetre, "Bruck's Battle," p. 26.

56   In October 2004, they were in . . . time she hit the ground.: Brian McGrory, "Completing Her Mission, *boston.com*, April 16, 2004, http://www.boston.com/sports/specials/marathon/articles/2004/04/16/completing-her-mission/.

56   Townsend plunged into depression . . . put his life back together.: Allen, Brown, and Regner, p. 297.

56   This is a matter of sudden change. I've got to adapt and look at this as a challenge.: Allen, Brown, and Regner, p. 297.

57   Watson was ranked among . . . day of his football career.: Kyle Meinke, "Steve Watson Sets Michigan Foot-

ball Record," *Ann Arbor.com*, April 24, 2012, http://annarbor.com/sports/um-football/journeyman-steve-watson.

57   He had known Watson . . . John McColgan was injured.: Meinke, "Steve Watson Sets Michigan Record."
57   "It's frustrating,": Meinke, "Steve Watson Sets Michigan Record."
57   When you start to feel . . . over again, that's hard.: Meinke, "Steve Watson Sets Michigan Record."
58   The temperature was ten . . . Wolverines arrived in Pasadena.: Cnockaert, p. 39.
58   Concerned about the heat . . . Yost practiced his team hard.: Cnockaert, pp. 39-40.
58   He tried to persuade Stanford's . . ten minutes each, but he refused.: Cnockaert, p. 40.
58   the game was scoreless for the first 22 minutes: Cnockaert, p. 41.
58   the Stanford coach asked Yost . . . The Wolverines accepted.: Cnockaert, p. 42.
58   Yost didn't use any of his three . . . have it known they hadn't played.: Rob Doster, ed., *Game Day* (Chicago: Triumph Books, 2006), p. 128.
59   his personal clock -- and thus . . . late to a team function.: Brandstatter, *Tales from Michigan Stadium Volume II*, p. 118.
59   On a trip for a Wisconsin . . . to get them out of trouble.: Brandstatter, *Tales from Michigan Stadium Volume II*, p. 119.
59   They told Schembechler they had . . . did nothing -- at the time.: Brandstatter, *Tales from Michigan Stadium Volume II*, p. 120.
59   at the team meeting on Sunday . . . the rest of the season: Brandstatter, *Tales from Michigan Stadium Volume II*, p. 121.
59   The worst thing you could do with Bo was be late.: Brandstatter, *Tales from Michigan Stadium Volume II*, p. 121.
60   When Michigan offered Matheny . . . who was on the field hockey team.: Daniel Wasserman, "Trading in Blue for Gold," *The Michigan Daily*, June 5, 2011, http://www.michigandaily.com/sports/trading-blue-gold.
60   God, I've asked you to be clear before, but c'mon.: Wasserman, "Trading in Blue for Gold."
61   In the '85 season opener against Notre, . . . for a two-yard loss.: Allen, Brown, and Regner, p. 257.
61   Attending an all-male school . . . to have a good time.": Allen, Brown, and Regner, p. 254.
61   When Messner landed in Detroit, . . . could see him play.: Allen, Brown, and Regner, p. 254.
61   The next morning, Messner called . . . "I'm a Wolverine.": Allen, Brown, and Regner, p. 255.
61   My dad was able to see my entire career. He died in 1989.: Allen, Brown, and Regner, p. 258.
62   who passed up the NFL to complete his degree: Jemele Hill, "Sweet Victory," *Detroit Free Press*, Jan. 2, 2001, p. A1.
62   With the game ball tucked . . . this their 10-month anniversary.: Hill, "Sweet Victory."
62   It was a spur-of-the-moment kind of thing.: Hill, "Sweet Victory."
63   Michigan head coach Lloyd Carr declared . . . was an incomplete pass.: Cantor, *Back on Top*, p. 99.
63   "There comes a time in which . . . whether it is a great team.": Cantor, *Back on Top*, p. 95.
63   In the locker room, Carr asked . . . "We all knew we could,": Cnockaert, p. 142.
63   Had Streets made a clean catch, he would have been short of the first down.: Cantor, *Back on Top*, p. 99.
64   "running on fumes,": "National Champs!" *MGoBlue.com*. http://www.mgoblue.com/sports/w-softbl/recaps/060805aaa.html.
64   Samantha Findlay became my hero.: Stephanie Wright, "With One Home Run, Samantha Findlay Became My Hero," *The Michigan Daily*, June 12, 2005, http://www.michigandaily.com/content/one-home-run.
65   As the team lined up, sophomore . . . that's what I do.": Michael Florek, "Fake Field Goal Gives Glanda a Shot at Glory," *The Michigan Daily*, Jan. 4. 2012, http://www.michigandaily.com/sports/fake-field-goal.
65   This is definitely the biggest catch of my life.: Florek, "Fake Field Goal."
66   when new head man Bo . . . activities, including their jobs.: Brandstatter, *Tales from Michigan Stadium*, p. 204.
66   Offensive line coach Jerry Hanlon did the checking on Brandstatter.: Brandstatter, *Tales from Michigan Stadium*, p. 205.
66   One summer the lineman worked . . . coach was not real happy.: Brandstatter, *Tales from Michigan Stadium*, p. 206.
66   Two weeks before he was to . . . "I am somewhat impressed,": Brandstatter, *Tales from Michigan Stadium*, pp. 206-07.
66   I was just chunky.: Brandstatter, *Tales from Michigan Stadium*, p. 204.
67   Kim played in the final . . . an 8-foot putt for the win.: Kevin Raftery, "A Roar from the Darkness," *The Michigan Daily*, April 17, 2011, http://www.michigandaily.com/sports/lion-kim-feature.
67   Now it's official. . . . an invite to the Masters.: Raftery, "A Roar from the Darkness."
68   by playing on at center . . . the ball with his left hand.: William F. Reed, "Big Man on Campus," *Sports Illustrated*, Nov. 9, 1992, http://sportsillustrated.cnn.com/vault/article/magazine/MAG1004475/index.htm.
68   Offense line coach Les Miles . . . sideline and I'll be fine.: Reed, "Big Man on Campus."
68   "I was trying to tell everyone . . . while the game was on TV.: Brandstatter, *Tales from Michigan Stadium Volume II*, p. 69.
68   During his senior year, . . . had backed out into his mouth.: Brandstatter, *Tales from Michigan Stadium Volume II*, pp. 69-70.
68   After that, his dad always said his son had a screw loose.: Reed, "Big Man on Campus."
68   I don't know whether . . . than most guys.: Brandstatter, *Tales from Michigan Stadium Volume II*, p. 69.

69 Lytle recalled that at the . . . in the mesh of the jersey.: Allen, Brown, and Regner, p. 162.

69 "a purely selfish matter . . . misfortune or frustration": Bruce T. Dahlberg, "Anger," *The Interpreter's Diction-ary of the Bible* (Nashville: Abingdon Press, 1962), Vol. 1, p. 136.

69 I'll never forget Greg DenBoer running for his life.: Allen, Brown, and Regner, p. 162.

70 The morning of the game a full-fledged blizzard roared into Columbus.: Wilbur Snypp, *The Buckeyes* (Huntsville, AL: The Strode Publishers, 1974), p. 131.

70 The wind blasted everything and everybody at 40 miles an hour,: Snypp, p. 132.

70 blowing the snow so hard that it came down "horizontally.": Snypp, p. 131.

70 During the game, the temperature . . . pitched in to help.: Snypp, pp. 132-33.

70 The 50,000 or so fans who braved the weather: Snypp, p. 131.

70 many of whom covered . . . as a shield against the merciless wind: Snypp, p. 132.

70 the last half was "just a struggle for survival.": Cantor, *Michigan Football: Yesterday & Today*, p. 46.

70 There were times when you . . . what was happening out there.: Cantor, *Michigan Football: Yesterday & Today*, p. 46.

71 he was referred to as "The Lost . . . to play hockey for Michigan.": Everett Cook, "The Heart of Texas," *The Michigan Daily*, March 15, 2012, http://www.michigandaily.com/print/65840.

71 he had his son on skates . . . listened to country music.: Cook, "The Heart of Texas."

71 A tattoo on his right shoulder . . . the other is a Michigan flag.: Cook, "The Heart of Texas."

71 He's not a typical Michigan kid. He's still a Texan at heart.: Cook, "The Heart of Texas."

72 When UM legend Fielding Yost . . . every letterman he could find.: Cnockert, p. 5.

72 the best he could come . . . from Canada named Biff.: "Biff, the Michigan Wolverine," *Wikipedia, the free encyclopedia*, http://en.wikipedia.org/wiki/Biff,_the_Michigan_Wolverine.

72 In 1927, the Detroit Zoo . . . stadium during football games.: "Biff, the Michigan Wolverine."

72 "The live Wolverines were a disaster,": Brian Bennett, "A Mascot for Michigan?" *ESPN.com*, June 20, 2011, http://espn.go.com/blog/bigten/post/_/id/28167.

72 "when Biff was placed . . . in two with his teeth.": Bennett, "A Mascot for Michigan."

72 "It was obvious that the . . . were by no means friendly.": Cnockert, p. 5.

72 Equally a failure was an attempt . . . banned from the stadium: Bennett, "A Mascot for Michigan."

72 [Fielding] Yost had not accounted for . . . ferocity of the animals.: "Biff, the Michigan Wolverine."

73 He picked up that superstition . . . off by himself to pray.: Chantel Jennings, "Players Believe in Pregame Routines," *ESPN.com*, Dec. 21, 2011, http://espn.go.com/espn/print?id=7374245&type=story.

73 It's football, and a lot of superstition is wrapped up into the game.: Jennings, "Players Believe in Pregame Routines."

74 He tells the story of one . . . "we did call it a 'Sally.'": Brandstatter, *Tales from Michigan Stadium*, p. 5.

74 "We made big plays with the 'Sally' all the time.": Brandstatter, *Tales from Michigan Stadium*, p. 6.

74 You want to run the Sally?" Brandstatter, *Tales from Michigan Stadium*, p. 5.

75 When Albert Wistert told . . . the newsman couldn't believe it.: Allen, Brown, and Regner, p. 18.

75 Wistert's father, a Chicago police . . . to pay the medical bills.: Allen, Brown, and Regner, p. 18.

75 Wistert got in some football . . . as far as football was concerned.": Allen, Brown, and Regner, p. 19.

75 been invited to Michigan by . . . follow his brother to Michigan.: Allen, Brown, and Regner, p. 18.

75 head coach Fritz Crisler "despaired . . . ever becoming a football player.": Bob Carroll, "The Eagle Tackle Was Albert," *The Coffin Corner*, Vol. 13, No. 1, http://www.profootballresearchers.org/Coffin_Corner/13-01-414.pdf.

75 "the clumsiness was . . . strength and speed.": Carroll, "The Eagle Tackle Was Albert."

75 His chance came against . . . "I decided no more of that,": Allen, Brown, and Regner, p. 21.

75 I want to be an All-American like my brother, Whitey.: Allen, Brown, and Regner, p. 18.

76 The top ten list is taken from John U. Bacon, "Top Sports Moments of the Decade," *Michigan Today*, Jan. 13, 2010, http://michigantoday.umich.edu/2010/01/story.php?id=7580.

77 The Wolverines were 0-2 with . . . ever had was 34,500.: Scott Bell, "Strength and Honor," *The Michigan Daily*, Sept. 16, 2007, http://www.michigandaily.com/content/strength-and-honor.

77 It was an incredible privilege to be part of being here today.: Bell, "Strength and Honor."

78 Networks billed it as Judgment Day:: Cantor, *Back on Top*, p. 122.

78 "We don't have to prepare for . . . no reason to respect us.": Cantor, *Back on Top*, p. 121.

78 They tried a pass of a fake . . . Seven yard loss.: Cantor, *Back on Top*, pp. 125-26.

78 Michigan's defense blew their offense to smithereens.: Cantor, *Back on Top*, p. 125.

78 the biggest lead ever run up on a Joe Paterno team at Happy Valley.: Cantor, *Back on Top*, p. 126.

78 Any student who couldn't make . . . believe what they were seeing.: Cantor, *Back on Top*, p. 125.

79 Michigan opened the game with . . . headed back to the bench.: Brandstatter, *Tales from Michigan Stadium Volume II*, p. 75.

79 "There was an attempted coup," . . . pretty heated conversation.: Brandstatter, *Tales from Michigan Stadium Volume II*, pp. 75-76.

79 It was a mutiny from the offensive line.: Brandstatter, *Tales from Michigan Stadium Volume II*, p. 76.

80 During the Minnesota game of . . . when men were tough.": Brandstatter, *Tales from Michigan Stadium Volume II*, p. 110.

81 The account of the game comes from "2010 Game of the Year," *Michigan 2011 Baseball Yearbook*, p. 19, http://viewer.zmags.com/publication/043e6a66#/043e6a66.

81 It's amazing. Some of the . . . true of to be a Christian man.: Jim & Julie S. Bettinger, *The Book of Bowden*

(Nashville: TowleHouse Publishing, 2001), p. 121.

82   In 1978, the freshman tailback . . . Davis changed all that,: Brandstatter, *Tales from Michigan Stadium Volume II*, p. 83.

82   He was so unknown his name . . . about the whole thing,": Brandstatter, *Tales from Michigan Stadium Volume II*, p. 84.

82   It got to me when I . . . It was really, really scary.: Brandstatter, *Tales from Michigan Stadium Volume II*, p. 84.

83   he was called to active duty . . . found by a local partisan: Ron Fimrite, "A Call to Arms," *Sports Illustrated Classic*, Fall 1991, p. 107.

83   sheltered them in a pink . . . didn't turn the Americans in.: Fimrite, "A Call to Arms," p. 108.

83   Despite weight loss from his confinement,: Fimrite, "A Call to Arms," p. 109.

83   I don't think I've ever wanted a relationship to succeed more than that one.: Fimrite, "A Call to Arms," p. 108.

84   He got his first chance to . . . whole season sitting on the bench.: Stephanie Wright, "David Is Goliath," *The Michigan Daily*, Nov. 3, 2006, http://www.michigandaily.com/content/david-goliath.

84   A year after the injury, . . . sit out four more games: Wright, "David Is Goliath."

84   You don't give your body time . . . than was originally done.: Wright, "David Is Goliath."

85   and ranked dead last in . . . the major statistical categories.: Alex Prosperi, "Facing 17-Point Halftime Deficit, Michigan Ousts Indiana in Overtime," *The Michigan Daily*, Jan. 7, 2009, http://www.michigandaily.com/content/2000-01-08/escape-bloomington.

85   "We played a terrible first . . . over the backboard.: Prosperi, "Facing 17-Point Halftime Deficit."

85   At the buzzer, Beilein "grabbed . . . "We didn't quit,": Prosperi, "Facing 17-Point Halftime Deficit."

85   they still trailed by six with . . . a trey to tie the game: Prosperi, "Facing 17-Point Halftime Deficit."

86   If you want it, you'll have to come up and win it.": Doster, ed., *Game Day: Michigan Football*, p. 123.

86   After his team arrived . . . the players' drinking water.: Tim Hyland, "The Little Brown Jug," *About.com*, http://collegefootball.about.com/od/traditions/p/trad-jug.htm.

86   Since he didn't trust his . . . cost the team 30 cents.: Doster, ed., *Game Day: Michigan Football*, p. 122.

86   "celebrated as though they . . . but to call the game.: Hyland, "The Little Brown Jug."

86   the Michigan players hurried to . . . come up and win it.": Doster, ed., *Game Day: Michigan Football*, p. 123.

86   The rivalry has been a . . . playing annually in 1929.: Doster, ed., *Game Day: Michigan Football*, p. 124.

87   head coach Bennie Osterman . . . and earned a letter.: Brandstatter, *Tales from Michigan Stadium Volume II*, p. 159.

87   I was sitting on the bench with tears running down my face.: Brandstatter, *Tales from Michigan Stadium Volume II*, p. 159.

88   The first time Seymour . . . better get outta here.": Brandstatter, *Tales from Michigan Stadium Volume II*, p. 122.

88   Early in the game, Tom Goss . . . "Where am I?" Brandstatter, *Tales from Michigan Stadium Volume II*, p. 122.

88   Seymour pondered his situation . . . was doing playing football.: Brandstatter, *Tales from Michigan Stadium Volume II*, pp. 122-23.

89   "perhaps the most unlikely star . . . until the war was over,": John U. Bacon, "Unassuming, Skillful, Swift," *attheplate.com*, http://www.attheplate.com/wcbl/profile_wakabayashi_mel.html.

89   "It was a good life," . . . He scouted Wakabayashi: John U. Bacon, "Unassuming, Skillful, Swift."

89   If you coach for 25 . . . for Christ, that is success.: Susie Magill, "'Coales' of Wisdom," *Sharing the Victory*, March 2009. http://www.sharingthevictory.com/vsItemDisplay.1sp?method=display&objectid=09 AC87.

90   *Time* magazine said they ran . . . flit about like wraiths.": Cnockaert, p. 59.

90   While many other college . . . out of seven different formations.: Cantor, *Michigan Football*, p. 39.

90   he is generally credited with giving birth to two-platoon football.: Tim Cohane, "The Man Who Modernized Football," in *Hail to the Victors* (Louisville, KY: AdCraft Sports Marketing, 1995), p. 88.

90   when the Magicians went out . . . Irish its "official" champ.: Cantor, *Michigan Football*, p. 39.

91   "Hey, you've been through this once before.": Nicholas J. Cotsonika, "Ziemann Ready for Final Season," *Detroit Free Press*, April 19, 1999, p. D2.

91   Ziemann pulled to his right . . . his senior year of football.: Cotsonika, "Ziemann Ready for Final Season."

92   Please, God, let me do something to make a difference.": Brandstatter, *Tales from Michigan Stadium Volume II*, p. 82.

92   "Slowly but surely, Michigan . . . Schembechler changed the play: Brandstatter, *Tales from Michigan Stadium Volume II*, p. 82.

92   who got a block from wide . . . never will forget that moment.": Brandstatter, *Tales from Michigan Stadium Volume II*, p. 83.

92   I remember raising my hands . . . scored to thank God.: Brandstatter, *Tales from Michigan Stadium Volume II*, p. 83.

93   Mark Rosen was playing collegiate . . . a date or just volleyball,": Eric Ambinder, "When Mark Met Leisa . . .," *The Michigan Daily*, Oct. 5, 2003, http://www.michigandaily.com/content/when-mark-met-leisa."

93   We come around a . . . her mom and her club coach.: Ambinder, "When Mark Met Leisa . . . ."

94   "We're going to be jacked up and we're going to win.": Emmanuel, p. 119.

94   "He's 22 years old, so he can say whatever he wants,": Emmanuel, p. 119.

94   "The game is played on the . . . "guarantee" scrawled across it.: Emmanuel, p. 119.

94   "I'd have said it myself if I had any guts.": Emmanuel, p. 123.

94   I knew if I made that kind of statement, I would have to back it up.: Emmanuel, p. 120.

95   Baas started high school as . . . "You come with me.": Allen, Brown, and Regner, p. 346.

95   He had hurt a knee late . . . whether he was any good or not.: Allen, Brown, and Regner, p. 348.

95   Baas came to Ann Arbor as a . . . "for possibly a week,": Allen, Brown, and Regner, p. 349.

95   He got his first start in 2002 as . . . Navarre got sacked.: Allen, Brown, and Regner, p. 348.

95   The week before the fourth game, . . . coaches asked Baas to move to center.: Allen, Brown, and Regner, p. 349.

95   You have to go in there. We have plenty of confidence in you.: Allen, Brown, and Regner, p. 349.

96   Bo Schembechler knew one thing . . . they were soft.: Cantor, *Michigan Football: Yesterday & Today*, p. 62.

96   Schembechler ran "ferocious practices . . . [the players] had never experienced.: Cantor, *Michigan Football: Yesterday & Today*, p. 62.

96   "We got after it in practice,": Brandstatter, *Tales from Michigan Stadium*, p. 6.

96   Schembechler carried a yardstick . . . would never be outhit.": Cantor, *Michigan Football*, p. 63.

96   "the walk-ons quit in droves." . . . who stay will be champions: Cantor, *Michigan Football*, p. 62.

96   During a scrimmage, he . . . the field still strangely quiet.: Brandstatter, *Tales from Michigan Stadium*, p. 6.

96   He looked around at . . . killed any ordinary human!": Brandstatter, *Tales from Michigan Stadium*, pp. 6-7.

96   Our practices were not for the faint of heart.: Brandstatter, *Tales from Michigan Stadium*, p. 6.

97   The program was hemorrhaging . . . either the trouble or the expense.: Zach Helfand, "On Hold," *The Michigan Daily*, March 22, 2012, http://www.michigandaily.com/sports/streak-year-and-phone-call.

97   Bacon called the selection . . . years of success were sown,": Helfand, "On Hold."

97   I felt devastated. I just think we were shafted.: Helfand, "On Hold."

98   Crisler "took Michigan into the . . . in the school's football history.": Cantor, *Michigan Football*, p. 31.

98   At the time, some teams . . . the helmet maize and blue.: "University of MichiganFootball: Michigan's Winged Helmet," http://bentley.umich.edu/athdept/football/helmet/mhelmet.htm.

98   His offense was based on a . . . an immediate visual clue.: Cantor, *Michigan Football*, p. 31.

98   The helmet debuted . . . cut interceptions in half.: "University of Michigan Football: Michigan's Winged Helmet."

98   Through all the changes . . . style to Michigan's look.: "University of Michigan Football: Michigan's Winged Helmet."

99   At his news conference on . . . they had at that position.: Kyle Meinke, "Michigan Coach Brady Hoke Says Vincent Smith 'Has Earned' Right to Be Lead Tailback," *Ann Arbor.com*, Sept. 19, 2011, http://www.annarbor.com/sports/um-football.

99   [I'll do] whatever I have to for the team to help them out.: Chantel Jennings, "Vincent Smith Puts on Variety Show," *ESPN.com*, Oct. 1, 2011, http://espn.go.com/colleges/michigan/football/story/_/id/7044342.

100   the Philadelphia Phillies threw a . . . to talk to my son.": Allen, Brown, and Regner, p. 191.

100   He told Rick if the money . . . believe in what he told me,": Allen, Brown, and Regner, p. 192.

100   He could barely walk and . . . we both just started crying,": Allen, Brown, and Regner, p. 193.

100   "That's one of the special moments I'll have till I go,": Allen, Brown, and Regner, p. 194.

100   It was the culmination of the end.: Allen, Brown, and Regner, p. 194.

WOLVERINES

BIBLIOGRAPHY

"1879 Michigan Wolverines Football Team." *Wikipedia, the free encyclopedia*. http://en.wikipedia.org/wiki/1879_Michigan_Wolverines_football_team.

"2010 Game of the Year." *Michigan 2011 Baseball Yearbook*. 19. http://viewer.zmags.com/publication/043e6a66#/043e6a66.

Allen, Kevin, Nate Brown, and Art Regner. *What It Means to Be a Wolverine: Michigan's Greatest Players Talk About Michigan Football*. Chicago: Triumph Books, 2005.

Ambinder, Eric. "When Mark Met Leisa . . . ." *The Michigan Daily*. 5 Oct. 2003. http://www.michigandaily.com/content/when-mark-met-leisa.

Bacon, John U. "Lucky Man." *Michigan Today*. 14 April 2009. http://michigantoday.umich.edu/2009/04/abbott.php.

---. "Michigan's Hockey Cinderella." *The Ann Arbor Chronicle*. 15 April 2011. http://annarborchronicle.com/2011/04/15/column-michigan-hockeys-cinderella.

---. "Top Sports Moments of the Decade." *Michigan Today*. 13 Jan. 2010. http://michigantoday.umich.edu/2010/01/story.php?id=7580.

---. "Unassuming, Skillful, Swift, Smart, Gentlemanly: They All Add Up to: Little Mel." *attheplate.com*. http://www.attheplate.com/wcbl/profile_wakabayashi_mel.html.

---. "Why Bo Didn't Go: Wisconsin's Treatment of Schembechler Had Long-Term Impact." *The Ann Arbor Chronicle*. 19 Nov. 2010. http://annarborchronicle.com/2010/11/19/column-why-bo-didn't-go.

Barnas, Jo-Ann. "Hendricks and Family Have U-M Tales to Tell." *Detroit Free Press*. 9 Sept. 1999. D1.

Baumgardner, Nick. "Now Is the Time for Michigan Basketball Team." *Ann Arbor.com*. 13 Feb. 2012. http://www.annarbor.com/sports/um-basketball/michigan-basketball-team.

Bell, Scott. "Rocking the Crable." *The Michigan Daily*. 26 Oct. 2006. http://www.michigandaily.com/content/rocking-crable.

---. "Strength and Honor: Crowe Inspires Blue." *The Michigan Daily*. 16 Sept. 2007. http://www.michigandaily.com/content/strength-and-honor.

Bennett, Brian. "A Mascot for Michigan." *ESPN.com*. 20 June 2011. http://espn.go.com/blog/bigten/post/_/id/28167.

Bettinger, Jim & Julie S. *The Book of Bowden*. Nashville: TowleHouse Publishing, 2001.

"Biff, the Michigan Wolverine." *Wikipedia, the free encyclopedia*. http://en.wikipedia.org/wiki/Biff,_the_Michigan_Wolverine.

Bigelow, Pete. "From 'Never' to Walking: Brock Mealer Will Lead Michigan Football Team onto Field Saturday." *AnnArbor.com*. 2 Sept. 2010. http://www.annarbor.com/sports/um-football/from-never-to-walking.

"Bo Schembechler." *Wikipedia, the free encylopedia*. http://en.wikipedia.org/wiki/Bo_Schembechler.

Brandstatter, Jim. *Tales from Michigan Stadium*. Champaign, IL: Sports Publishing L.L.C., 2002.

---. *Tales from Michigan Stadium Volume II*. Champaign, IL: Sports Publishing L.L.C., 2005.

Cantor, George. *Back on Top: The University of Michigan's Odyssey to the National Championship*. Dallas: Taylor Publishing Company, 1998.

---. *Michigan Football: Yesterday & Today*. Lincolnwood, IL: West Side Publishing, 2008.

Carroll, Bob. "The Eagle Tackle Was Albert." *The Coffin Corner*. Vol. 13, No. 1. http://www.profootballresearchers.org/Coffin_Corner/13-01-414.pdf.

Cnockaert, Jim. *Stadium Stories: Michigan Wolverines*. Guilford, CN: The Globe Pequot Press, 2003.

Cohane, Tim. "The Man Who Modernized Football." in *Hail to the Victors*. Louisville, KY: AdCraft Sports Marketing, 1995. 88-92.

Cook, Everett. "The Heart of Texas: How Ann Arbor Became Home for Chris Brown." *The Michigan Daily*. 15 March 2012. http://www.michigandaily.com/print/65840.

Cotsonika, Nicholas J. "Ziemann Ready for Final Season." *Detroit Free Press*. 19 April 1999. D2.

Dahlberg, Bruce T. "Anger." *The Interpreter's Dictionary of the Bible*. Nashville: Abingdon Press, 1962. Vol. 1. 135-137.

Doster, Rob, ed. *Game Day Michigan Fooball: The Greatest Games, Players, Coaches and Teams in the Glorious Tradition of Wolverine Football*. Chicago: Triumph Books, 2006.

"Elroy Hirsch." *Wikipedia, the free encyclopedia*. http://en.wikipedia.org/wiki/Elroy_Hirsch.

Emmanuel, Greg. *The 100-Yard War: Inside the 100-Year-Old Michigan-Ohio State Football Rivalry*. Hoboken, NJ: John Wiley & Sons, Inc., 2004.

Estes, Ben. "Let the Ball Talk: Twenty-Five Seasons of the Beilein Offense." *The Michigan Daily*. 28 March 2012. http://www.michigandaily.com/sports/let-ball-talk.

---. "Wolverines Hold On to Top Penn State, Earn Share of Big Ten Title." *The Michigan Daily*. 4 March 2012. http://www.michigandaily.com/sports/wolverines-hold.

"Facilities: Michigan Stadium." *MGoBlue.com*. http://www.mgoblue.com/facilities/michigan-stadium.html.

Fimrite, Ron. "A Call to Arms." *Sports Illustrated Classic*. Fall 1991. 98-109.

Florek, Michael. "Fake Field Goal Gives Glanda a Shot at Glory." *The Michigan Daily*. 4 Jan. 2012. http://www.michigandaily.com/sports/fake-field-goal.

Florjancic, Matt. "Fight of a Lifetime: Bruck Hasn't Let Diabetes Stop Her." *The Chronicle-Telegram*. 19 Jan. 2011. http://chronicle.northcoastnow.com/2011/01/19/fight-of-a-lifetime.

Gerstner, Joanne C. "Carmen Reynolds: Converting a Closet from Red to Blue." *MGOBLUE.COM*. 23 Nov. 2011. http://www.mgoblue.com/sports.w-baskbl/spec-rel/112311aad.html.

---. "The Accidental All-American." *M Magazine*. Winter 2010. 26-27. http://viewer.zmags.com/publication/a016c4aa#/016c4aa/26.

"Gophers Allow 28-7 Lead to Escape." *ESPN.com*. 10 Oct. 2003. http://scors.espn.go.com/ncf/recap?gameid=232840135.

Helfand, Zach. "On Hold: The Call That Birthed the Modern Michigan Dynasty." *The Michigan Daily*. 22 March 2012. http://www.michigandaily.com/sports/streak-year-and-phone-call.

Hersch, Hank. "That Great Abbott Switch." *Sports Illustrated*. 25 May 1987. http://sportsillustated.cnn.com/vault/article/magazine/MAG1065994/index.htm.

Hill, Jemele. "Sweet Victory: Thomas Caps a Record-Setting Career with Special Moment." *Detroit Free Press*. 2 Jan. 2001. A1.

Horgea, Brian. "Clock Ticking for U-M's Pollock." *MLive.com*. 28 Dec. 2007. http://blog.mlive.com/wolverines.stories/2007/12/clock-ticking.

Hyland, Tim. "The Little Brown Jug." *About.com*. http://collegefootball.about.com/od/traditions/p/trad-jug.htm.

Jennings, Chantel. "Players Believe in Pregame Routines." *ESPN.com*. 21 Dec. 2011. http://espn.go.com/espn/print?id=
  7374245&type=story.

---. "Vincent Smith Puts on Variety Show." *ESPN.com*. 1 Oct. 2011. http://espn.go.com/colleges/michigan/football/story/_/
  id/7044342.

Kartje, Ryan. "Michigan Runs Historic Winning Streak to 16 with Last-Minute Victory." *The Michigan Daily*. 24 March 2008.
  http://www.michigandaily.com/content/michigan-runs.

Lawrence, Andrew. "What a Run." *Sports Illustrated*. 22 Aug. 2008. http://sportsillustrated.cnn.com/vault/article/magazine/
  MAG1152245/index.htm.

Layden, Tim. "Double Threat." *Sports Illustrated*. 18 Nov. 1996. 44-47, 50.

---. "Prayer Answered." *Sports Illustrated*. 23 Sept. 1996. 44-46, 49.

Lopresti, Mike. "Michigan Leaves Notre Dame Feeling Blue." *USATODAY.com*. 12 Sept. 2011. http://www.usatoday.com/sports/
  columnist/lopresti/story/2011-09-11.

MacArthur, John. *Twelve Ordinary Men*. Nashville: W Publishing Group, 2002.

Magill, Susie. "'Coales' of Wisdom." *Sharing the Victory*. March 2009. http://www.sharingthevictory.com/vsItemDisplay.1sp?me
  thod=display&objectid=09AC87.

Maxwell, Fredric Alan. "The Late Great 98." *Michigan Today*. 17 Sept. 2008. http://michigantoday.umich.edu/2008/09/harmon.
  php.

McGrory, Brian. "Completing Her Mission." *boston.com*. 16 April 2004. http://www.boston.com/sports/specials/marathon/
  articles/2004/04/16/completing-her-mission/.

Meinke, Kyle. "Michigan Coach Brady Hoke Says Vincent Smith 'Has Earned' Right to Be Lead Tailback." *Ann Arbor.com*. 19
  Sept. 2011. http://www.annarbor.com/sports/um-football.

---. "Michigan Receiver Drew Dileo Is Headed Home to Land of Gators and Gumbo for Sugar Bowl." *Ann Arbor.com*. 25 Dec.
  2011. http://www.annarbor.com/sports/um-football.

---. "Steve Watson Sets Michigan Football Record for Positions Played, Looking for Just 1 in NFL." *Ann Arbor. com*. 24 April
  2012. http://www.annarbor.com/sports/um-football/journeyman-steve-watson.

"Michigan Scores with 2 Seconds Left, Stuns Irish." *ESPN.com*. 10 Sept. 2011. http://scores.espn.go.com/ncf/recap?gameId=
  312530130.

Murphy, Austin. "Shock Value." *Sports Illustrated*. 25 Sept. 2006. http://sportsillustrated.cnn.com/vault/article/magazine/
  MAG1105534/index.htm.

"National Champs! Findlay Drives Michigan Past UCLA." *MGoBlue.com*. http://www.mgoblue.com/sports/w-softbl/recaps/
  060805aaa.html.

Nesbitt, Stephen J. "The Strongest Muscle: The Backstory That Built Dave Molk into Michigan's Mainstay." *The Michigan Daily*.
  26 Oct. 2011. http://www.michigandaily.com/print/62746.

O'Neil, Dana. "Steve Fisher Had Success as a Sudden Interim Coach." *ESPN.com*. 22 Feb. 2008. http://sports.espn.go.com/ncb/
  columns/story?columnist=oneil_dana&id-3259425.

"Origins of the Michigan Band." *Michigan Marching Band*. http://mmb.music.umich.edu/node/43349.

Prosperi, Alex. "Facing 17-Point Halftime Deficit, Michigan Ousts Indiana in Overtime." *The Michigan Daily*. 7 Jan. 2009. http://
  www.michigandaily.com/content/2009-01-08/escape-bloomington.

Pyzik, Zak. "Split Decisions: Carmen Reynolds' Path from Buckeye Country to the Maize and Blue Nation." *The Michigan Daily
  News*. 15 Feb. 2010. http://www.michigandaily.com/content/carmen-reynolds.

Raftery, Kevin. "A Roar from the Darkness: Lion Kim's Journey to the Bright Lights of the Masters." *The Michigan Daily*. 17
  April 2011. http://www.michigandaily.com/sports/lion-kim-feature.

Reed, William F. "Big Man on Campus." *Sports Illustrated*. 9 Nov. 1992. http://sportsillustrated.cnn.com/vault/article/magazine/
  MAG1004475/index.htm.

Rohan, Tim. "A Humble Beginning." *The Michigan Daily*. 12 Feb. 2012. http://www.michigandaily.com/sports/sportsmonday-
  column-humble-beginning.

Rowland, Tom. "Michigan Snaps M.S.U. Jinx with 17-10 Victory." *Hail to the Victors*. Francis J. Fitzgerald, ed. Louisville, KY:
  AdCraft Sports Marketing, 1995. 109-112.

Rudner, Brad. "Soccer's Holly Hein: Determined to Win Another Battle." *M Magazine*. Fall 2011. http://viewer.zmags.com/pub-
  lication/a016c4aa#/a016c411/24.

Singer, Matt. "Pollock's TD Well-Earned." *The Michigan Daily*. 13 Sept. 2006. http://www.michigandaily.com/content/pollocks-
  td-well-earned.

Slovin, Matt. "Overtime Goal Sends 'M' Soccer to First-Ever College Cup." *The Michigan Daily*. 4 Dec. 2010. http://www.
  michigandaily.com/content/overtime-goal.

Snypp, Wilbur. *The Buckeyes: A Story of Ohio State Football*. Huntsville, AL: The Strode Publishers, 1974.

"University of Michigan Football: Michigan's Winged Helmet." http://bentley.umich.edu/athdept/football/helmet/mhelmet.
  htm.

VanMetre, Sarah. "Bruck's Battle." *M Magazine*. Fall 2011. 26-27. http://viewer.zmags.com/publication/4ea8b96d#/4ea8b96d/26.

Wasserman, Daniel. "Trading in Blue for Gold: Mike Matheny's Path to and from Michigan." *The Michigan Daily*. 5 June 2011.
  http://michigandaily.com/sports/trading-blue-gold.

Whitesall, Amy. "Be the Boat." *M Magazine*. Fall 2011. 14-16. http://viewer.zmags.com/publication/4ea8b96d#/4ea8b96d/14.

---. "Impossible Is Nothing." *M Magazine*. Fall 2010. 12-15. http://viewer.zmags.com/publication/e9add83c#/e9add83c.

Wright, Kevin. "Riley Excelling at Tackle." *The Michigan Daily*. 25 Sept. 2006. http://www.michigandaily.com/content/riley-
  excelling-tackle.

Wright, Stephanie. "David Is Goliath." *The Michigan Daily*. 3 Nov. 2006. http://www.michigandaily.com/content/david-goliath.

---. "With One Home Run, Samantha Findlay Became My Hero." *The Michigan Daily*. 12 June 2005. http://www.michigandaily.
  com/content/one-home-run.

WOLVERINES

INDEX
(LAST NAME, DEVOTION DAY NUMBER)

213

214